Memories in Translation

Memories in Translation

A Life between the Lines of Arabic Literature

Denys Johnson-Davies

With a foreword by
Naguib Mahfouz

The American University in Cairo Press
Cairo ≈ New York

To Paola who, beside much else,
has provided most of the photographs

The American University in Cairo Press
113 Sharia Kasr el Aini, Cairo, Egypt
420 Fifth Avenue, New York, NY 10018
www.aucpress.com

Dar el Kutub No. 2841/05
ISBN 978 977 424 938 9

2 3 4 5 6 7 8 9 10 14 13 12 11 10 09

Printed in Egypt

Foreword
by Naguib Mahfouz

It is really good to be translated and to be read both nationally and internationally . . . something great! Denys Johnson-Davies, whom I have known and admired since 1945, was the first person to translate my work—a short story—and he has since translated several books of mine, so I owe him a special debt of gratitude. In fact, he has done more than anybody to translate modern Arabic fiction into English and promote it. He has always sought out interesting new writers and worked hard not only to translate their novels, plays, short stories, and poetry but to find publishers for the translations too.

We have both advanced a few years since Denys translated that first short story of mine, and now is a good time for him to look back over a long and distinguished career, and to tell the story of how he came to be the leading English translator of modern Arabic writing, and of some of the writers he came to know along the way. I am very pleased that Denys has written this most interesting book, and I wish the reader as much pleasure in reading the book as I have had in knowing its author for sixty years.

1

An unlikely set of circumstances set me on the path to studying Arabic. Having spent a childhood firstly in Cairo, then in Wadi Halfa in Sudan, and finally in Uganda and Kenya, I went back to England on doctor's orders alone at the age of twelve, following a bout of amebic dysentery. Several months later my parents joined me, and after passing an entrance exam I soon experienced the unpleasant taste of boarding at a minor public school. It had been decided that I should study classics, and I was quickly twenty-third in a class of twenty-five. I had found that both Latin and Greek held few joys for me and that, furthermore, I found them extremely difficult—as well as basically uninteresting, because no one, it seemed, spoke them. Aged fourteen, I was expected to take my matriculation exams in the summer, though my reports had indicated that I was unlikely to pass and would have to spend the following year in the same class.

School provided little pleasure and a certain amount of pain, caning being practiced freely. The thought of having a further four or so years of this heartless routine appalled me. Even sports provided no respite, rugby being played in icy conditions—I never got used to England's climate—while cricket bored me except for the short periods when I was batting. Only two activities helped to rescue me from total tedium: the first was that palm-aching game known as fives, which I learned at the school and at which I represented the under-sixteens. This meant that every now and again I would escape through the gates and be taken to play at some other school, which invariably meant having an excellent tea and cakes after the match had been played. The one snag about the game is that it is played between four walls, with one's hands—inadequately clothed in special gloves—and a small, hard ball. My hands inevitably became bruised and could be protected only through placing slivers of raw beef inside the gloves.

The other game at which I showed some prowess was squash. I had played it before going to the school, my mother having put out the money for me to have lessons from a professional. Thus, despite my age, I was suddenly the champion of the school. But this happy state of affairs ended when—because the two squash courts were continually booked, and a number of the older boys were unable to find an empty court—a rule was posted up that the courts were only to be available for boys over the age of sixteen. When I informed my parents of this I was surprised to find my father, who had no interest in sport, waxing indignant at the thought that his son should be prevented from playing the game at which he excelled. Taking me back to school the next term, he went to see the headmaster with the idea of having me made an exception to the new rule. The headmaster, however, declared himself unable to make any exceptions: a rule was a rule. My father, already disappointed at my poor showing in Latin and Greek and at the fact that I would be required to repeat the year, presented the headmaster with an ultimatum: either his son would be allowed to play squash or he would be taken away from school. The headmaster rather pertinently asked what my father proposed to do with me if I was withdrawn—but my father answered that that was his business.

And so at the age of fourteen I found that something I hadn't even dared dream about had occurred: I was to be removed from school. My father then asked me what would I now like to do. "I would like to study Arabic," I was heard to reply immediately, as though the thought had been brewing in my mind for some time. In fact, no such thought had ever occurred to me—and little did I know at that time that the Arabic I would study was, like Latin and Greek, a classical language, with an even more developed grammar. Though as a child in Wadi Halfa, growing up with Sudanese children, I had spoken fluent Arabic, I had long forgotten every word—as a child one learns a language quickly but forgets it with equal ease. I suppose I had felt that my father would be pleased at such a suggestion, for he had himself started off at university studying Hebrew, Aramaic, and Syriac before the war intervened and he changed to law. In fact, my father—the son of an impecunious parson—had succeeded in getting to Cambridge only by learning while at school that a scholarship in Hebrew existed that would earn him a place at the university. With little more than a knowledge of the alphabet, he had been the only candidate for the scholarship, and was awarded it.

But my situation was not that simple. My father had put himself in a difficult position, as it would not now be easy to find me a place in some other school. Before making any further decisions about my future, it was essential that I now got seriously down to work in order to pass the examination for which the school had predicted I needed another full year. The only solution was for me to work hard at a crammer's in Birmingham (where we then lived) until the summer, when I could go up to Cambridge to take the examination known as Little-Go. Success in this exam would entitle me to go to a place at St. Catharine's, my father's old college. And so, aware of the risk my father had taken in removing me from school at such an early age, I devoted myself to preparing for the dreaded examination.

When I went to Cambridge with my father to take the examination, we stayed at his old college. A boy still not fifteen, I found myself among young men three and four years older, who were due to go up to the university the following September. My few days taking the exam were not without incident: on the very first morning, being in a highly nervous state, I found myself unable to unbolt the door on the lavatory, and eventually got out only by climbing through the narrow gap at the top of the door—I thus sat down several minutes late for the first paper!

Though I passed the exam, the college told my father that I could not be admitted to go up at the age of fifteen. Exceptionally, however, I would be given a place at sixteen. Special arrangements were therefore made for me to spend a year at the School of Oriental Studies in London before going on to Cambridge. As for the summer, it was decided that I should go to Cairo, where it was thought I could at least learn the Arabic alphabet. Arrangements were made for me to stay with an Egyptian who had been a lecturer at the School of Oriental Studies. I suppose, having returned from East Africa to England on my own at the age of twelve, I wasn't daunted by the prospect of going out to Egypt on my own.

The person in whose flat I was to stay—his name was Abdul Raziq—lived in an area called Sakakini, not one of Cairo's more elite districts. Little of it remains in my mind except the address at which I had stayed. During the intervening years between then and now I had been curious to go back and see the place, and only last year it suddenly occurred to me to suggest to my friend Said al-Kafrawi that we drive there. He happened to know the district, but assured me that no street by the name I mentioned existed. However, my memory of some sixty-five years proved to be right, and a house was found to be still intact at 12, Sharia Sa'id.

Sakakini had little to attract me, so almost daily I would take the tram to central Cairo, where I would sit around in the cafés and watch the world pass by. One of my few memories of those times was my embarrassment at boarding a tram, witlessly seating myself in a compartment reserved for women, and being ignominiously escorted out by the ticket collector.

One night in Sakakini I woke up to a sound of crepitation, and found that my bed was alive with cockroaches. Despite the protests of my host that my father had arranged for me to be there for the length of my stay in Cairo, I took myself off to the Pension Suisse in downtown Antikkhana, where I would at least be near Groppi's and the other cafés I frequented. As it happened it was a good move, in that I made friends with a young Yorkshireman by the name of Wilf Smithson, who lived in the same pension and took pity on the lonely English boy who had suddenly appeared there. Some ten years older than myself, he was the Middle East representative of a pharmaceutical firm that produced Nivea cream. Wilf possessed a car and knew the city well. We went horse-riding several times out at the Pyramids, and would often spend the evening at one of the city's open-air summer cinemas. After a successful life as a businessman in various parts of the world, he retired to Geneva, where he acquired Swiss nationality. In my many wanderings I would often pass through Geneva and stay with Wilf and his wife Frances, while they sometimes stayed with me at my seaside house in Salobrena, south of Granada. It was there, some fifty years later, that I first noticed a change in his behavior, as he became a victim to Alzheimer's disease. One of my saddest memories is of seeing him in his flat in Geneva demanding angrily of Frances about me: "Who's this person who's sitting around the flat all the time?"

Whereas my stay in Cairo was enjoyable enough, my copy of Thatcher's *Arabic Grammar* remained scarcely opened. I had tried my hand rather unsuccessfully at the alphabet and had read with dread about the case endings, the unwritten short vowels, the dual number, the subjunctive and jussive moods, and the almost infinite variety of irregular noun plurals. Time enough for all that, I thought, when I got to university.

The School of Oriental Studies at that time was housed in an old building in Vandon Street in Victoria. It required the Second World War to persuade the powers-that-be that eastern languages were worth encouraging, and a fine new building was later made available in Bloomsbury for what was renamed the School of Oriental and African Studies. Such fellow students as I had consisted for the most part of foreigners: among them was the Egyptian sheikh Abdul Aziz al-Maraghi; a professor from Valetta University called Joseph Aqualina, who wrote poetry and befriended me; America's present leading Arabist Bernard Lewis, who is said to advise George W. Bush and his colleagues; an Iraqi called al-Douri; and several Indians. There were also other students studying Sanskrit, for instance, and Tibetan. Most of them seemed to be postgraduate students, and the total student population seemed to number no more than a few dozen. Being some ten years younger than anyone else, I was sadly out of things; also, there seemed to be no classes for beginners in Arabic, though eventually a certain Sheikh Mohamed Mahmoud Gomaa (who was later to be a colleague at the BBC) introduced me to the intricacies of Arabic grammar, while somebody else showed me how much easier an Indo-European language like Persian was than Semitic Arabic.

During most of my time in London I stayed in a small flat in Dolphin Square, a large block that had recently been erected in Pimlico on the Thames. There were several hundred flats in the block, and the main feature that interested me were the several squash courts, with their own professional and his assistant. I still recollect that the professional's name was Tom Land; his young assistant was generally accompanied by a greyhound. Several times I went with him of an evening to one of the stadiums to see the dog race. He knew many of the other owners and trainers, and I would sometimes risk the odd few shillings on a race—watching dog races, which are over in a matter of seconds, is less boring when one is betting on one of the dogs. I remember once when my friend's dog seemed to be winning, a man in the audience threw down a cushion in exasperation among the runners, and the race was declared null and void.

I suffered from loneliness during my time in London, for my fellow students were all much older than myself, and I knew no one else; weekends were especially difficult. I would often go down to the courts and watch people play or would eagerly await a call from Tom Land to tell me that somebody wanted to have a game and was looking for someone to play with: was I free? Much of the time I spent reading, and I remember particularly the effect that a volume of the collected stories of D.H. Lawrence had on me—heady stuff for a fifteen-year-old. Sometimes my father would have to come down to London on business from Birmingham and would join me in the flat. We invariably went out to dinner at a steak house and then on to one of the music halls that were the vogue in those days and which my father enjoyed.

On going up to Cambridge the following year, I was ill-equipped for reading such texts as the *Kamil* of al-Mubarrad and various extracts from the Qur'an. I was also horrified to learn that it had been decided that for my second language I should study Hebrew rather than Persian. Used to getting my own way in most things, I was informed that a proper understanding of Arabic could only be obtained with a knowledge of Hebrew—though I know many Arabs with an excellent knowledge of their own language who know not a single word of Hebrew. This was a battle that I lost, largely because I was not qualified to argue the case, but also owing to the fact my father had himself previously studied Hebrew with a certain Professor Loewe, who happened to be still at Cambridge and who would be my teacher of Hebrew. I made very heavy weather of both Hebrew and my teacher. Very early on he told me that on coming across the word *Yahweh*, the sacred name of God that should never be pronounced, I should say instead *Adonai*, which means 'my Lord.' This I consistently failed to do, not through any bloody-mindedness on my part but simply because I was continually stumbling over the Hebrew letters. My initial dislike of Hebrew was brought about by the realization that, while Arabic and Persian had the mystery of providing keys to texts otherwise inaccessible, the only texts available in Hebrew appeared to be those one was already familiar with through one's reading of the Bible—though, when it came to it, much of the translation of the Old Testament seemed to relate only vaguely to the original Hebrew. I well remember the outsized dictionary called Brown, Driver, and Briggs, which I was constantly consulting and which, with the lesser known words, gave suggested meanings and other instances in the Old Testament where they had appeared and their possible meanings in the various contexts.

For my bad luck—I was, incidentally, the only student studying Arabic and Hebrew for the First Part of the Oriental Language Tripos—I was also required to read, as part of the set books for Arabic, portions of the Qur'an with Professor Loewe. I still have my notes for the Chapter of the Cave, and find them bespattered with Hebrew words—one of Professor Loewe's theories being that both the Arabic language and the Qur'an itself were derived largely from Hebrew and the Old Testament.

During the time I was at Cambridge—a total of five terms—the only other students studying Arabic were Abba Eban (later to become Israel's minister of foreign affairs), who was several years senior to me and was, I think, taking a doctorate; Geoffrey Bibby, who attended one or two classes of Arabic with me and specialized in Assyrian, later becoming a well-known archaeologist and carrying out excavations of the burial mounds of Dilmun on the island of Bahrain; and Stephen Naish, whose father was a Quaker and had been a missionary in Lebanon.

It came as no surprise when the end-of-year results showed that I had failed in Hebrew. After I had completed one unsuccessful year at Cambridge, a war—as had previously happened with my father—came to my rescue. There seemed to be no money for me to continue my studies, so I applied for a job with the Censorship Department in Liverpool. I was accepted, presumably on the basis of my having studied Arabic for two years. However, when it came to it, I was quite incapable of reading even the simplest letter in Arabic—reading Arabic handwriting requires more knowledge than one acquires at a university—yet I stayed on for two or three months censoring letters in English until someone discovered that I was too young to be employed there at all. In the meantime, my mother had come in for some money from her mother, and she generously decided to use some of it so that I could continue at Cambridge.

I was determined, whatever happened, not to pursue my unsuccessful studies of Hebrew, and announced that I was going to change to Persian. I was told that as I had not taken Persian in my first year, it was out of the question for me to try to cover two years of Persian in two terms (I had already lost one term by working at the Censorship). However, no doubt Professor Loewe had similar feelings about me to mine about him and was glad not to have to go on teaching Hebrew to someone so set against it. It was thus agreed that after all I could change to Persian.

Good fortune came my way in the shape of two teachers of Persian who immediately inspired me with a love for the language and its literature. Both were professors from the School of Oriental Studies, which had been moved up to Cambridge because of the war: one was the well-known Russian scholar Vladimir Minorsky, the other Hasan Taqizadeh, who I think had previously been Persian ambassador in London. Another reason why the choice of Persian as a second language was a happy one was that I had a good friend in an Indian (this was before Partition) with whom I shared rooms when I was in London: Mohamed Anwar's father at one time had been the personal doctor to the then king of Afghanistan, and Mohamed himself was to have a distinguished career as a lawyer in Pakistan. He was strongly anti-Hindu, and knew Rahmet Ali, who is credited with first thinking up the idea of a Muslim homeland and calling it Pakistan.

Mohamed Anwar knew Persian well, including much erotic verse by the Indian Mohamed Iqbal, who wrote in both Urdu and Persian, and he went through with me the whole of the portion of Saadi's *Bustan* that had been prescribed. He particularly admired the poetry of Hafiz, and to this day—while scarcely able to say 'good morning' in Persian—I can still quote many lines from his *Diwan*. The parts of Firdowsi's *Shahnameh* that had to be read I did with Professor Minorsky, who made the experience of reading this difficult ancient poet less of a drudge than it might have been, by providing me as we went along with all sorts of sidelight information about such subjects as Zoroastrianism and the history of Persia before the coming of Islam. Meanwhile the *Chahar Maqaleh*, the only prose work set (Persian literature consists largely of poetry), I did with Taqizadeh.

I continued with Arabic but was dogged by the feeling that I was being taught a dead language, yet another Latin, which put me off. One of my troubles was that my teachers of Arabic—who included the great Professor Nicholson, so well versed in the literature of Sufism and the translator of Jalaluddin Rumi's Persian masterpiece the *Masnawi*—had never, to the best of my knowledge, visited anywhere in the Arab world and their interest in it was confined to its past. Nicholson was an old man by the time he was giving me private lessons during one winter in a freezing cold top room in a building in Bateman Street. It didn't seem to be his home, as the building had all the appearance of being deserted and the room, I recollect, was almost devoid of furniture. He was by then retired and gave me lessons in composition and dictation. I had the impression—I hope wrong—that he was in need of the few pounds he made from giving me private lessons. I remember little about this remarkable man except that, when giving me dictation, he pronounced Arabic with a heavy English accent and that the intense cold in the room caused his nose to drip.

My other teacher of Arabic was Professor Storey, a man of extreme shyness with a very high-pitched voice. By this time I had been joined in my Arabic classes by Stephen Naish. It was with Professor Storey that Stephen and I read the *Kamil* of al-Mubarrad. The two of us sat at a large table around which, for the hour of the lesson, Professor Storey circumambulated. His way was blocked by a wire that went from a radio that sat on the table to the socket in the wall. Each time Professor Storey reached the wire he would raise it above his head and duck under it. Stephen and I lightened the boredom of the lesson by keeping track of the number of times he made it around the table. Then, as we came toward the end of term, Professor Storey suggested that during the coming holiday we should learn German, a language that he said was essential for anyone studying Arabic. Needless to say, neither of us paid any attention to our teacher's injunction. However, during our first class the following term, there was a reference in our text to some personality of the period, and Professor Storey brought down the massive German encylopedia and asked me to read aloud the article indicated. It must have been obvious to Professor Storey that I understood not a word of what I stumbled over, but he merely remarked, in his flute-like voice, that we were now all properly informed about So-and-so, and simply returned the book to its place on the shelf.

Before attending a lesson, we were required to prepare one or two pages of the *Kamil*. On one occasion, Stephen and I found to our delight that during our next lesson we would be dealing with a passage containing a description of an attempted assassination, in which the unfortunate victim had his penis cut off. We were eager to see how Professor Storey would deal with this, but when we came to the passage he commented that we had all no doubt looked up any words we didn't happen to know and that we could now continue on to the next page.

Having no teachers who had Arabic as their native tongue, and no text that remotely looked like modern Arabic, I was left wondering what sort of language the Arabs of today spoke and in what language their newspapers and magazines were written. I remembered meeting David Cowan, who was among several students of the School of Oriental Studies who had transferred to Cambridge because of the war. He had lived in Cairo for several years, had become a Muslim, had studied at al-Azhar University, and was later to compile a grammar that would be published by Cambridge University Press and would replace Thatcher's *Arabic Grammar*. I recollect once being invited to tea at his digs and seeing a copy of an Arabic magazine lying around, and being impressed at his ability to read it. Despite his unusual command of Arabic, he did not have a particularly successful academic career and was never appointed beyond the position of reader. The reason for this was that he had not troubled to take a doctorate and had not produced the myriad scholarly articles and books that are a sine qua non for advancement in the academic world.

The fact that the School of Oriental Studies had moved up to Cambridge meant that a number of interesting people were made available. Another person who became a friend of mine at that time was A.L. Basham, who was studying Sanskrit. He was a poet and had published a novel about English country life, of which he gave me a copy, writing the dedication in Sanskrit, in Devanagari script. He was later to become professor of Indian history at the School of Oriental Studies and to write a monumental work on the subject. I also got to know John Blofeld well, a Sinologist and the translator of numerous Buddhist texts, as well as a book on the Tao, of which he gave me a copy. He was later to move to Bangkok, where he taught at the university. When later working for a firm of consulting engineers I one day found myself in Abu Dhabi, and—with an interest in Buddhism—I was able to exchange my first-class return ticket to London for a tourist ticket that took me to London via Bangkok. There I spent a week with John and became aware of how ill-qualified I was to understand the cultural background to Buddhism, with no knowledge of Pali, Sanskrit, Tibetan, Chinese, or Japanese. An unlikely person I got to know during this period was Musa Husseini, who was later to be hanged for organizing the assassination of King Abdullah of Jordan. I remember sharing a punt with him on the Cam—could this amiable man really be the same Musa Husseini?

The person I spent most of my time with in Cambridge was Geoffrey Bawa. He was also a member of St. Catharine's College, and liked it no better than I did. At that time St. Catharine's was well known for its excellence in sports, and a predominance of the members of the rugby team were 'Cats' men. I well recollect being summoned to see my tutor, T.R. Henn, an expert on W.B. Yeats, who had been a brigadier in the war. He reminded me that an exception had been made in my case to allow me up to Cambridge so early, and that I should therefore do my best to conform. It seems that I was not to be seen following the progress of the St Catharine's boat in the 'Bumps' that were a yearly feature of rowing on the River Cam. I answered—quite reasonably, I thought—that I was not interested in rowing. I was then told that even if I wasn't interested, I should at least show some interest when my college's boat was involved. I was later to be in further trouble with my tutor when, having been given a place in the college squash team, I failed to make a place in the university team, and excused myself from continuing to play for my college. Dr. Henn asked me about this, and I gave the unsatisfactory answer that I had become bored with squash.

Socially, I spent most of my time with Geoffrey Bawa and his group of friends. He was from Ceylon and flouted the fact that he was gay. He dressed in flamboyant style and spent as little time as possible in the college. He was taking English, but not very seriously, and was failed in his Anglo-Saxon paper. However, academic success at Cambridge was not important to him as he came from an affluent background. He later became a barrister and practiced law for a while in London. Understandably, he did not enjoy it. I, too, at a much later date, studied law and found the experience of 'being at the bar' equally distasteful. Though not interested in making an academic success of English, Geoffrey was widely read in literature, and it was from him that I learned of such writers as Cocteau and Gide, both of whom he got to know during visits to Paris. With my general education interrupted at an early age, Geoffrey exercised a good influence over me in introducing me to various authors who might have remained unread. I later heard that, on returning to Colombo, he had become an architect and had specialized in landscape gardening. Then, only last year, I was staying at the Royal Overseas League club in London and was skimming through their magazine when I saw an article about Geoffrey Bawa having been awarded the Agha Khan prize for architecture. I immediately wrote to him, and had a reply from someone working for him to tell me that for several years he had been paralyzed by a stroke.

When the results came out, it seems I passed adequately in Arabic and did well in Persian. Even so, Professor Nicholson had already expressed serious doubts about the chances of my being able to make a living out of Arabic. As he rightly pointed out, there were only three or four academic posts in England to be filled by Arabists, and my record so far hardly qualified me for a place in academia. I had enjoyed studying Persian, and would have liked to continue with it, but if there was no possible career for me with Arabic how would I fare any better with Persian?

I had so far taken only Part One of the Tripos and still had the second part to take. In the circumstances it seemed pointless to carry on with Arabic—I had looked at the set books for Part Two and found them mind-bogglingly difficult and dull. I therefore decided to change to anthropology, and began reading some books on the subject. I don't know how I thought that anthropology would provide me with a career any more than oriental languages would. When I first took up Arabic, it had not occurred to me to ask myself what sort of career I could pursue with it. I still find myself, at my present age, asking young people in their teens what they plan to do with their lives and knowing full well that, for the most part, they have not the slightest idea and simply want to get on with the present and let the future look after itself. All I felt sure about was that I didn't want either an office job or one that required me to spend time in England.

2

In the event, I was saved from making a decision by a call from the BBC, asking me to go for an interview with the Arabic section. Arabic had been the first foreign language in which the corporation, as from 1938, had started to broadcast. I turned up at Broadcasting House, where I was interviewed by various people and was then taken to a studio to hear a news bulletin. Nobody questioned me about what I had made of the bulletin of which I had scarcely understood a word. I was surprised to be told that I would be taken on as a trainee and that I should stay in London until I was contacted. I remained in my digs in Earl's Court with my Indian friends, while the air-raid warnings sounded nightly and the occasional bomb disturbed our games of three-handed bridge.

For a time I felt that I had been forgotten and that the BBC had changed their minds about employing me, then came a call asking me to report at the Arabic Intelligence Department in a small village called South Newington, not far from Evesham. There I found that my boss was Nevill Barbour, an Arabist who had written one of the earliest books about the Palestine question under the title *Nisi Dominus* and who was also the author of a book about Morocco. He was one of the few Arabists who had an interest in the burgeoning renaissance in Arabic literature, and he had made translations of some of the writings of the playwright Tewfik al-Hakim. Other people working in the department included L.P. Elwell-Sutton, who had written a grammar of colloquial Persian and was employed as the first editor of the BBC's magazine *al-Mustami' al-'arabi* ('The Arabic Listener').

There seemed to be nothing for me to do in the Arabic Intelligence Department, which despite its name was concerned solely with analyzing letters from listeners and replying to them, so I did nothing. I enjoyed becoming acquainted with the surrounding countryside, though I did express my doubts about the fairness of paying me a mere three pounds a week while I was required to pay out three guineas for my board with breakfast and supper; I pointed out that under this arrangement I was three shillings a week out of pocket and had still not had lunch, smoked a cigarette, or drunk a glass of beer. As I was billeted on Nevill Barbour and his wife in their beautiful country house, he should have been aware of the unfairness of my position. When I complained, I was told that I was lucky not to be in the army. Even at that early age not noted for my tact, I replied somewhat tartly that in the army I would get free board and lodging and at least something in the way of pocket money. At this early stage in my life I was discovering that organizations like the BBC—and later the British Council—require handling with a certain calculated adroitness if one is not to be exploited.

Eventually it was decided to send me to Evesham, from where the actual broadcasts in Arabic were made. My new boss was the Arabic program organizer, E. H. Paxton, known for his translation of the first volume of Taha Hussein's autobiography, under the title *An Egyptian Childhood*, one of the very earliest books from modern Arabic to be published in English translation. I remember him telling me that the book had sold a mere two hundred copies. Many years later, when I had started up the Arab Authors series with Heinemann, I republished the translation; it is now continuing life in an edition produced by the AUC Press that also includes the later two volumes that make up Taha Hussein's autobiography. One is of course merely stating the obvious in saying that one's life crisscrosses: one Christmas, Paxton and his wife invited me to

Christmas lunch, at which I met his small son, Julian; some thirty years later, invited by an Omani friend to visit his country, I was met at Muscat airport by a large, bearded man who introduced himself as Julian Paxton!

My duties at Evesham included what was known as switch censorship, especially of the main evening transmission, which included not only a news bulletin but cultural talks and music. Switch censorship meant being in the studio with the broadcaster and cutting him off the air if he were suddenly to begin spouting anti-British sentiments. The task of switch censorship having been assigned to me, the rest of the English staff were free to go home at a reasonable hour and be with their families. My other duties included the checking of translations made into Arabic of talks to be broadcast, and reading through scripts from other services and choosing those I considered suitable for being broadcast in Arabic; these I was then required to shorten and adapt. Additionally, together with my boss, I would read and comment on any scripts that were submitted for broadcast.

What surprised me greatly was that, apart from some twenty Arabs, not a soul in the Arabic section of the BBC could be said to have more than a superficial command of the language. How was it that Britain had acquired this great empire, which included a large number of people whose native language was Arabic, and yet appeared to boast virtually no one who knew the language? I remember, later on, David Cowan telling me that, given the job of testing the ex-members of the Sudan Political Service (of which at one time my father had been a member), he had found not a single person who knew anything better than kitchen Arabic, although all of them had been required to pass examinations in the language. And how was it that the BBC was successful in its special application to have me—a reasonably healthy young man of eighteen, with virtually no experience of the Arab world—exempted from military service on the basis of my knowledge of Arabic? Were there no old dodderers who had served their time in the Arab world and were capable of performing such duties? The fact that for most of the time I was at Cambridge I was the only person studying Arabic hardly shows—as suggested for example in Edward Said's bestseller *Orientalism*—that Britain was busy training people to study Arabic so that they could become spies and so forth. At that time no attempt was made to teach Arabic other than as a dead classical language. It took the war itself to show that Britain possessed virtually no Arabists, or people with any knowledge of other oriental languages, and it was only then that the government arranged for special scholarships to be given to those willing to take up such languages.

So indispensable, it seems, was I for the BBC that even when my father pulled several strings from Cairo—where he had been transferred to the military mission to the Egyptian army—to have me given a commission in Army Intelligence, this was successfully resisted by the corporation.

For me my five years with the Arabic section of the BBC amounted to a period of attendance, as it were, at a third university—a university where my studies were more concentrated than they had so far been, in that for most of my waking hours I practiced Arabic, at the hands of Arabs, in both its written and spoken forms.

For a time I shared an office with my boss. Then came the time when I bought myself a large cherrywood pipe and began smoking a herbal mixture, which was much cheaper than tobacco. The choking bush fire that resulted meant that I was soon found an office to myself, complete with an attractive young secretary, who turned up daily with a large black cat in a basket. I have never been known for my tidiness, but the black cat further increased the chaotic state of the office, with its saucers of milk and toilet tray.

The Arabs, mostly Egyptian, employed as broadcasters, translators, and typists, had chosen for the most part to be housed in one of the Nissen huts set up in the same area as the offices and studios. This saved them from making the daily trip by special bus into the somewhat dull town of Evesham, where one could be billeted. I myself had initially been automatically billeted in the town. I found myself in the same house as a Moroccan Jew named Leon Abulafia; he was the person nearest to me in age in the department, and we became good friends. He had been born in the seaside town of Mogador in Morocco, a town with a large community of Jews, and had spent most of his life there; his father had been in the tea trade. I heard a lot about his early life in Mogador, little knowing that more than fifty years on I would come to know Mogador well under the new name it had been given of Essaouira. While Leon spoke Moroccan Arabic fluently, he could neither read nor write the language. The BBC, realizing that many Moroccans were unable at that time to follow a news bulletin in the classical language, had decided to have several newscasts in the colloquial Moroccan dialect. For this purpose they hired three Moroccans from the Free French forces. None of these, however, spoke any English, and so Leon had been employed to translate and dictate the news bulletins to them—also, as best he could, to see that they didn't get into any trouble, for they were a rough trio. One day I remember walking with Leon all the way from Evesham to the offices and studios: it was a Saturday and, being an Orthodox Jew, he refused to take the bus, and I accompanied him on the walk. This I soon regretted as it came on to rain, and on we trudged; the bus came by and the driver stopped for us, looking in disbelief as we both turned down the offer of a lift!

The advantages of transferring to the Nissen hut were only too obvious. My English bosses showed their disapproval, but it turned out to be one of the best decisions I have ever made. Not only was I in walking distance of work and the 24-hour canteen, but I found myself housed with some twenty Arabs who naturally didn't stop conversing among themselves in Arabic just because a young Englishman was now living among them. Intrigued by my seeming determination to learn Arabic, several of them went out of their way to help me. I was persuaded to keep one notebook in which I wrote down words that were new to me; another notebook contained lines of poetry and of *zagal* (poetry in the colloquial language); while a third notebook was devoted to recording proverbs in the Egyptian dialect. In the evenings I would sit around, following as best I could their conversation and asking for the meaning of words or phrases I didn't know. Gradually I found myself understanding more and more, and after a time I ventured to utter the odd sentence. Evenings were generally spent playing poker, often into the early hours of the morning so that the session would break up and everyone would go off for an early breakfast before snatching a few hours of sleep. I would sit up with them and follow the game being played, with large sums of money being won and lost. I then began playing and became addicted, playing each night to win or lose more than my meager monthly salary. All of them, of course, earned considerably more than I did, and I understood why gambling is forbidden in Islam and saw how it affected several of my colleagues. One of them had to sell his car, and another left England and returned to Egypt in flight from the money-lenders to whom he fell in debt.

What gambling could do to a man was vividly illustrated to me some twenty-five years later. I had returned to England from the Middle East and had become a lawyer. I was telephoned by a solicitor who said he had a client who had known me years back, and would I see him? It was somebody—not an Arab—who had from time to time joined our poker school. From playing poker he had graduated to playing the horses and was now in serious debt to several bookmakers and money-lenders, who were threatening to go to his bosses at the BBC, where he still worked. I gave him the only sensible advice I could, which was to go to his administrative chiefs at the BBC and tell them frankly about what was happening. The BBC backed him up and came to some arrangement on his behalf with his creditors, but some months later I heard from the same solicitors that he had borrowed a large sum of money from a friend and had lost it all on the horses; in despair he had then gone into Harrods and stolen some bulky object, which he had hidden under his coat. As he was leaving the store he was stopped, and ended up being prosecuted for theft. His solicitor felt that he had planned the whole thing so that he would be found out and now actually looked forward to a respite in prison away from his troubles.

As Arabic gradually became less of a closed book, I tried to find out whether there was any sort of literary renaissance in the Arab world. Were novels and short stories being written? I learned that the short story was being practiced by a small number of writers, the best known of whom was Mahmoud Teymour. As it happened, my father, while in

Cairo, had somehow met Mahmoud Teymour, who sent me several volumes of his short stories. I also became aware of the writings of Tewfik al-Hakim through my colleague Nevill Barbour. During this time I translated one or two of Teymour's short stories and was able to have them published in some of the 'little' magazines, such as *International Short Story* and *The Wind and the Rain*, that were being produced at that time.

In this context it is interesting to see what Sir Hamilton Gibb, one of the few Orientalists at that time who showed any interest in the literary renaissance, had to say about it in the revised second edition of his *Arabic Literature*, published in 1963: "All of these productions, however, short stories, novels and plays, remain bounded by the horizons and conventions of the Arab world; when translated into other languages they are often more interesting as social documents than as literary achievements."

I also began writing my own short stories, and was fortunate enough to find a literary agent by the name of Stephen Aske. The office appeared to be run by an elderly chain-smoker named Leslie Beresford, who went out of his way to encourage me with my writing. He achieved this mainly by doing all he could to sell any short stories I sent in to him, be it even in obscure publications coming out in Australia. Publication, anywhere, has always been a spur for me, ever aware that I was no literary genius. Putting manuscripts away in drawers has never appealed to me, nor yet the depressing chore of sending out manuscripts with stamped, addressed envelopes for their return. Several of my stories appeared in *Modern Reading*, but perhaps, oddly enough, the height of my achievement at that time was a rejection slip: it was from the prestigious American magazine *Story* to say how much they had enjoyed my story "The Last Defeat," which they were nonetheless, for various reasons, unable to publish. It was a story that was inspired by the number of cheerful young Italian prisoners-of-war, whom we would occasionally meet working in the surrounding countryside.

More than fifty years later I submitted some specimen stories to Quartet in London, and they agreed to publish a volume. The book, published under the title *Fate of a Prisoner*, received no notices except for a complimentary review in *Al-Ahram Weekly* by my friend John Rodenbeck of the American University in Cairo and—surprisingly—a more than generous piece in *The Literary Review* by the novelist Francis King, who was unknown to me except through his writings. This showed me how little chance an unknown writer had unless his publishers possessed the necessary 'clout' to influence notices in the media that counted.

During my years at the BBC I learned that there was a scholarship in Arabic at the School of Oriental Studies worth £50. I put in for it—and then heard that several people who had initially applied had withdrawn on hearing that someone working in the Arabic section of the BBC was also sitting for the scholarship examination! I thus found myself the only candidate, and I was duly awarded the Ouseley Memorial Scholarship. I was persuaded to take the Diploma of the School of Oriental Studies in Modern Arabic, which had recently been introduced.

The set books, as far as I can remember, were *al-Nazarat* by al-Manfaluti, a writer who wrote essays in a floridly sentimental style; a selection of poems by three 'modern' poets, the Egyptians Ahmad Shawqi and Hafiz Ibrahim and the Lebanese Khalil Mutran; and a volume of political and philosophical writings by Muhammad Abduh. I found myself unimpressed by any of them, though I now realize that Ahmed Shawqi is widely admired. Certainly, the set books in no way reflected anything that could be regarded as 'modern.' However, I took the examination and did, I thought, relatively well, except for the grammar paper, which I found almost incomprehensible. The questions in this paper were largely about the theory of Arabic grammar and included, I remember, one question asking what were the genders of certain words and why; while I was able to answer the first half of the question, I was at a loss to think up reasons for certain nouns being either masculine or feminine. On attending the interview following the exam, I was surprised to find that one of the examiners was Dr. Gamal al-Din Heyworth-Dunne, who had recently returned from Egypt, where he had held some important job liaising between the British army and the Egyptian government. He had the rare distinction of being able to speak Arabic fluently. It was he who had arranged for me, some years back, to stay with a former Egyptian lecturer at the School of Oriental Studies when I had visited Cairo in the summer of 1937. At the interview I was told that had I not scored so badly in the grammar paper I would have been awarded the diploma with distinction. I naturally asked what the answers were to the various questions in the grammar paper that I had been unable to complete and I remember being informed by Heyworth-Dunne that the answer to the question about the gender of certain words was to be found in a paper by a German Orientalist published in some learned German periodical. I expressed the opinion that I thought it was quite unreasonable to ask someone being examined for a general diploma in modern Arabic a question that required him to have read some article in a learned German journal. Nevertheless, I was awarded the diploma without distinction.

I was therefore greatly surprised when, a few weeks later, I was telephoned at work by Heyworth-Dunne and told what an excellent performance I had put up, and would I go round and have dinner with him and his wife Fatima at their flat in Hampstead? During dinner Heyworth-Dunne told me that a special Chair in Modern Arabic was being created for him, and that he had great plans for the School of Oriental Studies, which had for too long been in the hands of old-fashioned scholars, and that he wanted to introduce fresh blood into the Arabic department by employing people like myself. He told me that in order to pursue a successful academic career it was necessary for me to take a doctorate, to which I answered that I had neither the time nor the money. The question of money, he assured me, presented no difficulty as he could easily arrange for my scholarship to be extended for the period required. We then went on to discuss a possible subject for my doctoral thesis, which, he said, he would personally supervise. He then chose a subject relating to education in nineteenth-century Egypt (not a subject I would have chosen, but one about which he himself had written), and he sat down there and then and drafted a letter for me to send to the School. My application, he explained, would automatically be passed to him for approval.

I was amazed to receive a letter from the School some days later telling me that my application had been refused by Dr. Heyworth-Dunne because the subject I had chosen was unsuitable, and because my previous academic record did not qualify me for registering for a doctorate. I had already seen, during that one evening I had spent with Heyworth-Dunne, how obsessed he was with the failings of other English Arabists who might be regarded as possible rivals, but couldn't see that I fell into that category, being some twenty years his junior. What, then, was the point of his going to so much trouble to shoot me down when I hadn't yet taken to the air? I resolved then and there that academic life was not for me.

However, it so happened that some twenty years later, when I was living in London and had set up an office specializing in Arabic translation, I received a call from Bob Serjeant, with whom I had for a time overlapped at the BBC and who had taken over the Chair of Modern Arabic at the School of Oriental and African Studies, asking me to go and see him. At the meeting he asked me whether I would like the post of a lecturer at the School. He couldn't offer me a more senior post because of my lack of academic qualifications, but he thought that I might like to do some teaching of Arabic and that, in any case, I would not be required to give up running my translation business. The offer intrigued me and I accepted it. I then left his office and went along the corridor to the general Common Room where I met several people whom I knew slightly. On being asked what I was doing there, I replied that I had just seen Professor Serjeant and that I was joining the Arabic department. The dismay on the faces of those present at finding yet another possible rival to their advancement persuaded me to retrace my steps to Bob Serjeant's office and ask to be excused from accepting his kind offer. Thinking back on other forays into the academic world, I find that the only time when I really enjoyed it and felt wholly free from anxiety was when I spent a couple of years as a lecturer at the English Language Department of the then Fouad al-Awwal University in Cairo. The reason for my peace of mind there was that all my colleagues were working at the University in Cairo simply because they enjoyed living in Cairo, and entertained no ambitions to become more than what they were.

3

With the end of the war with Germany I was at last free to make a move from the BBC. I heard that there was a job with the British Council in Cairo to teach Arabic translation at the British Institute. I applied for it and was taken on. I was overjoyed both to leave the BBC and to escape the rigors of living in wartime England. On resigning I was told by my boss that I had made a big mistake and that a great future awaited me in the Arabic Section. I answered, in somewhat typical fashion, that if my past was anything to go by I was well out of the Corporation.

On the boat on which I traveled to Port Said was a colleague from the BBC, Abdel Salam Ali Nur, an Egyptian married to an Italian. He had studied art in Italy and was employed by the BBC as art editor of the magazine *al-Mustami' al-'arabi* ('The Arabic Listener'). He spent much of the trip making caricatures of our fellow passengers, and, once we had arrived in Cairo, introduced me to a number of his friends there. Many years later, when I returned to London and was editing the quarterly magazine *Aswat*, he provided some excellent pen-and-ink drawings for a short story by Tayeb Salih.

In Cairo I also looked up the critic and writer Louis Awad, with whom

I had overlapped for a short time at Cambridge. Through him I got to know several interesting intellectuals, among them the influential journalist and writer Mohamed Mandour. It seems that one day I was with Mohamed Mandour, perhaps also with Louis Awad, in the Groppi Garden and had been seen by my boss, the director of the British Institute. Thus one morning on arriving at the Institute, I was told that the director wished to see me. He started off by observing that I was spending too much time with Egyptian friends and that I should mix more with my English colleagues; he then went on to say that he had seen me at Groppi's with Mohamed Mandour and why hadn't I reported to him that I knew this important person? I answered that I had been employed to teach Arabic translation, not to act as a contact man with Egyptians who might be considered of interest.

While at the British Institute I got to know Fouad Munib and, through him, his mother, Mary Munib, who was a well-known comedy actress. She was a member of Nagib al-Rihani's company, which performed comedies in the colloquial language at the Ritz Theatre in Emad al-Din Street. I attended al-Rihani's last play, entitled *Silah al-yawm* ('The Weapon of Today'), being a satire on modern life in Cairo, and wrote about it on 15 June 1946 in *The Sphinx* as follows: "Nagib al-Rihani, as the central character, starts off life selling books round the cafés and, in a matter of months, with the help of a good deal of bluffing and wangling (not always of the most honest variety) ends up as the director of a large bank. Right at the end of the play, just when he has extricated himself from being charged with large-scale swindling, Nagib al-Rihani explains what 'the weapon of today' is. The simple formula for getting on in life is: 'If you're going to steal, do it on a big scale, and when you steal a loaf of bread remember to eat only a half or three-quarters and give the rest away to the right people, who will thus be indebted to you and will be compelled to help you when the inevitable catastrophe comes!'" Wouldn't this comedy relate equally well to today? Nagib al-Rihani not only acted in these comedies but collaborated in writing and directing them. I recollect that one of his plays was entitled *The Uninvited Guest*. To the audience it was quite clear who the uninvited guest was, and the

British Embassy soon raised objections to the play and it was taken off.

It should have come as no surprise to me when, having worked out my initial contract of two years, I found that my contract with the British Institute was not to be renewed. This was a blow to me as I had only recently married and could see no way in which I could stay on in Cairo. However, as one of the wisest verses in the Qur'an says: "Perhaps there is something that you dislike which is in fact best for you, and something you like which is worst for you." So it was that, one day, walking along on my own, I was greeted by a bearded man who accosted me with the words: "Aren't you the person whose services have been dispensed with by the British Council?" I admitted that yes, my contract was not being renewed. "Why don't you come and join us at the university?" he suggested. I replied that perhaps I didn't have the qualifications for teaching English at the university, as my studies had not included English literature at university level. "It's enough for me that you got thrown out of the British Council. I'm sure you'll make out fine." The man was Bryn Davies, professor of English at Fouad al-Awwal University, later to be called simply Cairo University.

I spent two happy years there, with several colleagues who became good friends, among them the novelist P.H. Newby, one of the earliest winners of the Booker Prize, the Muslim Arabist Martin Lings, also known as Siraj al-Din Abu Bakr, who wrote, among many other publications, the standard biography of the Prophet; the novelist Robert Liddell; and the poet Hilary Corke. There was also a lecturer named Crawford, with whom I would often play chess. Having resigned from the university in 1949, I was not later subjected to the unpleasantness of being removed from my job and sent out of the country, as happened to my colleagues when Nasser came to power. Instead, I continued to visit Egypt on a regular basis, and on one such visit I bumped into my old friend Crawford. Surprised to find him still in Cairo, I asked what he was now doing. "Oh, I'm still at the University," he answered. "But weren't you all thrown out?" I asked. He smiled and answered: "It seems you didn't know I'm Irish, not English."

While still at the British Council I worked on a book of short stories by Mahmoud Teymour. This writer, acknowledged as the pioneer writer of the Arabic short story, came from an aristocratic family of Turkish origin. I used to see him fairly regularly, either alone at the al-Gammal Café, which was almost opposite the British Institute, or at the lunches he used to organize for groups of budding writers, such lunches being generally held at al-Khumayyis or some other kebab restaurant. Teymour, despite his aristocratic background, was not one to frequent the large and expensive hotels. Through him and his group I got to know most of the younger writers of the day.

Once Teymour and I were having coffee on our own at al-Gammal. He always insisted on paying and I knew he could afford to—even so, he had the strange habit of taking out his packet of cigarettes and cutting a cigarette in half before inserting half in his holder and lighting it; no doubt it was an attempt to cut down on his smoking. At that time I too used to smoke, and I recollect that on that occasion a man selling combs and odds and ends passed by. Having waved him on, I realized that I was out of cigarettes, so I called him back and asked him to buy me a packet of Bahhari ('Sailorman'), as Players cigarettes were then known. The man took my ten piasters and came back with the packet of cigarettes and two piasters change, which I handed back to him. The man was adamant in refusing the money, and I turned to Teymour in disbelief. "I'll tell you why," he said, and called the man back. He then asked him how long it was since he had left his village and come to Cairo, to which the man answered that he had only recently arrived in the city. "You see," Teymour said to me. "But the city will soon steal his natural nobility from him."

Teymour was generous in his support of young writers, though he was very much of his generation, and was shocked when I showed him a short story by a friend that contained a description of a donkey urinating as it progressed along a dusty road. "This is not the stuff from which literature is made," he told me stiffly. He was regarded by many writers of the younger generation as viewing Egyptian life from an unreal angle and taking an almost touristic view of the characters from which he wove his stories. Having said which, it was largely by Teymour's efforts that the short story became the most popular genre of writing in Egypt for several decades.

Like every writer employing Arabic, he was preoccupied by the problems of whether the colloquial should be used in literature. At one time he wrote several plays in the colloquial language, comedies about local life. I found them amusing and thought that they came off well. Teymour, however, then decided he was doing a disservice to Arabic literature by employing the colloquial language and rewrote all the plays in classical Arabic. The result, in my opinion, was disastrous. All he succeeded in doing was to show that classical Arabic was wholly unsuitable as a vehicle for humor. Who has ever heard of anyone cracking a joke in the classical language—other than at the expense of that language? I remember once discussing with Teymour the problems of the writer faced with these two different languages, and his saying to me, "If God gives us life, we'll see that in fifty years every Egyptian will be talking classical Arabic." God gave at least one of us sufficient life to see whether, in fifty years, the classical language would take over. It quite obviously has not—in fact, with the deterioration in standards of education, fewer and fewer people in Egypt have a proper command of the classical language, and the trend must surely be—as with Latin and the romance languages—that the colloquial will gradually replace the classical. I appreciate that there are religious and political considerations that make this a delicate subject, one in which a foreigner should be careful how he treads, but wishful thinking is not enough to make the classical language prevail. Looking through a recent copy of the *Guardian Weekly*, I noticed an advertisement for various posts at the University of the United Arab Emirates, containing a note to the effect that all subjects other than Arabic and Islamic history were taught in English.

It is surely significant that writers of the caliber of Tewfik al-Hakim, Yahya Hakki, and Yusuf Idris have all employed the colloquial language in their writing, with Tayeb Salih sometimes even using colloquial Sudanese. Naguib Mahfouz, as is well known, eschews the colloquial language and makes even the least likely of his characters express himself in the classical language. However, when his novels are adapted for the screen his characters revert to their normal voices. In the late 1940s, before fame made it difficult for one to have a tête-à-tête with him at a café, we had discussed this question of language—and both of us remained unconvinced of the other's point of view. His was, quite simply, that classical Arabic was the language that every Arab reads, and that by introducing colloquial Egyptian, for example in the dialog, one might estrange non-Egyptian readers. As for Egyptian readers, they would automatically in their minds render the dialog into a suitable idiomatic colloquial. There is much to be said for that argument, and I recollect clearly my impatience with a novel by the talented Iraqi writer Fuad al-Takarli in which all the dialog was in colloquial Iraqi, and I found myself unable to finish reading it because of my lack of acquaintance with the dialect. I am nevertheless convinced that, for the Iraqi reader, the novel gained something by having the dialog in the colloquial.

To return to Teymour: Having already published one or two stories by him in magazines in England, I decided to read through all his production of short stories and select a sufficient number to make a small volume. I knew there was no question of finding a publisher for such a book—the American University in Cairo had yet to set up its publishing activities—and I was therefore obliged to produce it at my own expense under the imprint of the Renaissance Bookshop. Before taking it off to a printer, I decided to have someone look through the manuscript. This business of giving someone a manuscript to comment on is of course particularly difficult for the person consulted. Obviously, all the writer really wants is for the manuscript to be handed back a few days later with some congratulatory phrases. For my good fortune I gave it to a colleague at the Institute, a man who had himself published several books and whose opinion I valued. While initially I was upset by his frankness, he nevertheless gave me a valuable lesson in translation. On returning the manuscript of short stories, he made some complimentary remarks about the stories, but then added that the translation itself in some cases was not altogether in proper English. Shocked, I asked him to give me some instances, which he readily did. "But that's what the Arabic says," I protested. "I don't care what the Arabic says," he countered. "I as a reader happen not to know a single word of Arabic and all I care about is having a text that reads well in English. After all, translation is an art, and the role of the translator is to take in the original text, thoroughly digest it, and then regurgitate it in acceptable English. This is especially so where the language from which you are translating is so different from English."

I took his words to heart and went through the whole manuscript again before taking it to the printer. Abdel Rahman Azzam Pasha, secretary general of the Arab League at the time, wrote a short introduction to the volume. Produced in 1947, it was, I believe, the first volume of Arabic short stories to be published in English translation.

When I presented some copies to Mahmoud Teymour, he asked me, with his customary generosity, how much I had paid to have it printed and how much I would eventually make when all the copies had been sold, and he gave me a check for the total amount, remarking that he could afford to wait until the edition was sold out. There had previously been no suggestion that if I were to do a volume of his stories, he would pay the costs.

4

One of the leaders of the literary renaissance in Egypt was of course the playwright Tewfik al-Hakim. He had an office at *al-Ahram* newspaper, but I would sometimes sit with him of a morning at his favorite haunt on the street outside the Café Ritz at the bottom of Qasr al-Nil Street opposite the National Bank building. I had already read his *Yawmiyat nai'b fi-l-aryaf* ('Diary of a Country Prosecutor') and felt that it would be an amusing book to translate, and one that would test my translating abilities, especially as much of the dialog was in the colloquial language. However, when I approached him about this, he told me that regrettably during the war he had given such permission to Abba Eban, who was at that time a British army intelligence officer and was later to become Israel's minister of foreign affairs. The translation duly appeared under the title *The Maze of Justice* and is still in print.

Having read the novel in translation and enjoyed it, I decided to introduce it to the English-reading public through a talk to be given on ESB (Egyptian State Broadcasting), which included programs in English. (I was a regular contributor and I translated for them a number of short stories by the writers of the time, some of which were then published in *Cairo Calling*.) However, having written something to the effect that the novel portrayed the poverty in which all too many Egyptian peasants lived, I was surprised to find my words published in an Egyptian newspaper, *al-Zaman*, where I was accused of running down Egypt. On going one morning to the university, I was met with an enthusiastic reception from my students. "Bravo, it needed you, a foreigner, to have the courage to say such things." "What things?" I asked, not being a reader of newspapers. It was ridiculous to accuse me of criticizing Egypt in that, for one thing, we were living in a time of state censorship and my script had of course been passed. I was later informed that no less than King Farouk himself was furious about the matter and that steps were going to be taken to make me persona non grata in Egypt. This was the last thing I wanted and I racked my brains to see who I knew who could help me in this impasse: the name Yahya Hakki, writer, diplomat, and friend, immediately sprang to mind. I paid him a visit at the Ministry of Foreign Affairs, and he rang Edgar Gallad, the proprietor and editor of *al-Zaman*, who agreed to see me. In a state of high dudgeon, I went to see the man and threatened to bring an action against his paper if he didn't at once publish a refutation together with an apology. More a man of the world than I, he laughed in my face and informed me that the paper never published refutations, but promised, in due course, to publish an item in praise of myself and my services to Arabic literature, which he later did.

And so ended my second scrape with the powers-that-be. The first had come about through the weekly page I contributed to the magazine *The Sphinx*. The page consisted of several items mainly about Egyptian personalities, in an attempt to show the English reader of this *Tatler*-like publication that Cairo also contained some interesting Egyptians and wasn't solely inhabited by a small coterie of English people who were regularly holding tea parties. One week I had mentioned that some members of the English community had invited an Egyptian belly-dancer to perform. Fun was made of her and she was offended when several men in the audience sought to imitate her. I wrote that we English were guests in a foreign country and that we should respect all aspects of life around us. This, it seems, had enraged the British ambassador, and early one morning I found a military policeman at my door. When he asked me to accompany him to the embassy, I told him that I had no intention of doing so, but changed my mind when he pointed out that the ambassador himself was unhappy about something I had written and that he possessed the power to have me placed on a plane back to England. I was driven in a jeep to the embassy, which I now entered for the first time. I was met by a certain Major Sansom, who I was later to understand was a person of some influence in the country and who drew a gloomy picture of my predicament. I pointed out that the offending words had all been passed by the censorship, but this was not enough for him. He told me that the matter could perhaps be resolved by my writing a letter of apology to the ambassador. Would he, I asked, be so good as to dictate such a letter, as I had no idea what sort of document would placate the ambassador? There and then I wrote out in longhand the letter that Major Sansom dictated to me, and nothing further was heard of the incident. It did, however, show me how what I regarded as a trivial comment in a newspaper could have caused me considerable harm.

Tewfik al-Hakim had somehow attracted to himself a reputation for miserliness. I never had occasion to test this out, but it was a constant subject of joking among those who knew him. I often visited him in his office at *al-Ahram* and he always proved an entertaining companion. Having had his later education in France, he was of course fluent in French and well read in its literature. One day when I was visiting him at *al-Ahram*, he opened the drawer of his desk and produced, with evident glee, a letter from the great French Arabist Louis Massignon, famous for his study of the Sufi writer and martyr al-Hallaj. The letter, I was surprised to see, was written in Arabic and contained a number of grammatical errors, and it was these that Tewfik al-Hakim wanted to point out to me. Why, I asked myself, had Massignon risked writing in Arabic to someone he knew very well was perfectly able to read a letter in French? I myself studiously avoid writing in Arabic unless forced to do so, only too aware of the delight caused by any mistakes I might make.

It is, of course, primarily as a playwright that Tewfik al-Hakim is known. Finding that the novel I wished to work on had already been rendered into English, I set about translating several plays by him, although aware that plays in book form were not much in demand. The first of these to be published was one of his later works, a play of the absurd entitled *The Tree Climber*, which was published in a paperback edition by Oxford University Press. Local opinion about it had been mixed, though I see that today, so many years after it was written, it is still performed in Cairo. Another four plays—two full-length and two one-act—were then published in the Heinemann Arab Authors series under the title *The Fate of a Cockroach and Other Plays of Freedom*. I also included one of his one-act plays entitled *The Donkey Market* in a volume of Egyptian one-act plays, also produced in the Arab Authors series. The full-length play *The Sultan's Dilemma* was produced on the BBC Home Service radio, and recently found its way into an edition of Norton's *Masterpieces of the World*. Like all my translations from modern Arabic literature, none of these books made much money, either for me or for the author, the arrangement made by Heinemann being that author and translator divide the royalties fifty–fifty, with no advance. On the subject of monetary rewards, I remember Tewfik al-Hakim, on one of my visits to his office, opening the drawer of his desk and producing a check, which he waved in front of me. It was from Heinemann, the publishers of the Arab Authors series, and was for six months royalties: a total of £3.60. "It would be a real shame to cash this," he joked. "I think I'll get it framed so I can hang it up."

It was many years—nearly half a century—later that I was invited to lecture at a university in Syria. Before going in to address my audience I was asked by my host, the head of the English Department, what the subject of my talk would be—I think he was somewhat put out to find that I did not carry with me a sheaf of closely typed paper from which I would be reading, something that I myself find agonizingly off-putting when I am part of an audience. I told him that my general theme was something along the lines of "Translation Is an Art." He immediately riled and said: "Here we teach that translation is a science." We were obviously at odds before I had even started. "But surely," I protested, "the meaning of a word or phrase can change according to the context." "How do you mean?" he demanded. I rummaged through my mind and came up with: "For instance, in Arabic what you are sitting on is a *kursi* and this is normally translated as 'chair,' but in the Qur'an God does not sit on a chair but on a throne so that *Ayat al-Kursi* should be translated as 'The Verse of the Throne' rather than 'The Verse of the Chair.' Also, the word *kursi* happens to mean the 'seat' in a *goza* tobacco pipe where hashish smokers place the pellet of hashish." The man looked at me with disapproval, clearly wondering what sort of strange Orientalist I was. Then, just before I followed him into the lecture hall, he asked me which English university I was teaching at. I was met by a further look of disapproval when I answered that I lived in Egypt and didn't teach at a university.

Having finished my off-the-cuff piece (in English), I invited questions. One of the teaching staff then took me to task for translating the title of Tewfik al-Hakim's play as *The Sultan's Dilemma*, when what the playwright had actually written was 'The Perplexed Sultan.' It was pointed out to me that the Arabic title had contained a noun and an adjective, and that I should have rendered it in the same manner. I defended my rendering—after all, didn't 'The Sultan's Dilemma' both give the meaning and also make a more attractive title? I found that my student audience seemed to be on my side: I felt they had had enough of being taught translation as a science! I also found myself crossing swords with another of the teachers, who took me up on having mentioned that Jalaluddin Rumi, the great Sufi poet, wrote in Persian. He pointed out that the poet had lived in Konya in Turkey, and that it is there until today that the famous dervishes perform their dance. To this I replied that while he certainly lived and died in Konya, Jalaluddin Rumi had also certainly written in Persian, for I had studied the language at university and had read the great man's poetry in the original. While loath to put down a teacher in front of his students, who by now were employing Arabic in their exchanges with me, I had no choice but to defend myself. I was supposed to attend for a second afternoon at the university, but at the end of the session I was informed by the head of the department that something had cropped up that made it impossible for the students to be there.

5

Naguib Mahfouz I got to know during the time I spent in Cairo between 1945 and 1949. We would meet at one of the cafes he frequented, and early on I translated a story from his very first volume, *Hams al-junun*, to be broadcast on the English program of Cairo radio.

In about 1947 I read his novel *Zuqaq al-Midaqq*, and felt immediately that nothing like it had ever been written in Arabic. I remember going to one of Taha Hussein's weekly soirees with Louis Awad, and mentioning the book, to find that no one there had heard of Mahfouz or the novel. Fatma Moussa, one of Egypt's leading critics—and the mother of the novelist Ahdaf Soueif—recently reminded me how, when she was a student of mine at Fouad al-Awwal University, I had spoken to the class with enthusiasm about Naguib Mahfouz and *Zuqaq al-Midaqq*. Although I had certain reservations about it, I started to translate it and finished about a third of it before giving up, feeling that I would never find a publisher for it. However, the Canadian Arabist Trevor Le Gassick translated the book and published his translation in Beirut.

I know that Naguib Mahfouz entertained hopes that, as I had translated some of his short stories, I would in due course translate one of his novels, as he knew how much I admired his writing. Meeting in one of the cafés he frequented, we would often discuss his work. Never imagining that I was addressing a future Nobel prizewinner, I would criticize his novels, insisting, for instance, that a novel such as *The Thief and the Dogs* was lacking the degree of both sex and violence that English readers would expect from a novel with such a plot. I believe it is a sad reflection on British publishing that had Naguib Mahfouz not won the Nobel prize for literature in 1988 he would not have found a mainstream publisher for his work in English translation.

On one of my frequent visits to Cairo when I was living elsewhere in the Arab world in the 1980s, I learned that Naguib Mahfouz had signed a contract with Mark Linz, the director of the American University in Cairo Press, for the rights to translate his work into English. When I next met Naguib at the café, I asked him about this and expressed the hope that he had concluded a good deal with the Press. He told me that, in fact, he had entrusted his translation rights without any advance payment, and that he had also included the translation rights in all other languages. I was flabbergasted—and showed it. "And how many of my books have you published?" he asked with a smile. "At least this way I shall get some of my work translated and published in English and other languages." To this I had no answer, and his wisdom in concluding the foreign rights agreement was shown when, unexpectedly, he was awarded the Nobel prize—due in the main to nine of his novels having appeared in translation through the AUC Press, while one or two other titles appeared in the Arab Authors series that I had started with the British publishers Heinemann Educational.

The story of Naguib Mahfouz and the Nobel prize is an interesting one. During one of my visits to Cairo during the years when I was living in France or Spain, I received a call from a friend to say that the Swedish wife of the French ambassador to Tunisia was in Cairo and wished to see me. We met at the unlikely venue of the Cleopatra Hotel, where she told me that the committee was looking into the possibility of the Nobel prize being awarded to an Arab writer. She had with her a list of names of possible candidates, including the Syrian poet Adonis, the Egyptian short story writer Yusuf Idris, the Sudanese writer Tayeb Salih, and Naguib Mahfouz. She first asked me whether I felt there was any other writer from the Arab world who deserved to be considered, and, feeling that the list was complete, we discussed at length the relative merits of these possible candidates. Adonis could not be called a popular poet, and his decision to give up his actual Muslim name in favor of 'Adonis' did not endear him to many Arabs, quite apart from the fact that his poetry was above the heads of many readers; Yusuf Idris, though highly regarded as the leading exponent of the short story in the Arab world, did not have sufficient material available translated into either English or French, the two languages known to the members of the committee; Tayeb Salih at that time had only his novel *Season of Migration to the North*, the novella *The Wedding of Zein*, and some three or four short stories available in English and French, and this meager output ruled against his being awarded the prize—having been his translator into English, I would of course have been delighted if he were to win it. Discussing the merits of the various contenders, it was clear that Naguib Mahfouz was the favorite, not only because of the high quality of his writing but also because of the extraordinary number of novels and volumes of short stories he had produced. Though I was intrigued that consideration was being given to the possibility of an Arab writer, I thought nothing more about my meeting with the Swedish lady and was as surprised as Mahfouz himself was reported to have been when he was first told that he was to be awarded the prize.

While living in Beirut between 1970 and 1974, I was approached to join the team engaged in translating the novels of Naguib Mahfouz into English for publication by the AUC Press. It was felt that most translators did not possess a sufficiently good knowledge of both Arabic and English, and that therefore an initial translation should be undertaken by a native speaker of Arabic and that the translation should then be handed over to one or more persons who would 'iron out' the initial text. I refused to be part of this team, believing that, just as a book cannot normally be composed by a committee of several people, so too the translation of it should be left to one person. A look, for instance, at the title page of the Mahfouz novel *Miramar* reveals that no less than four names have participated in its translation—which is not to say that the end result is not perfectly acceptable. Whereas in my opinion not the ideal method of translation, the AUC Press project to translate works by Naguib Mahfouz did produce a number of translations of his novels, and it was due to the fact that there was a sizeable body of his work available in English that he won the Nobel prize.

I was responsible for recommending to the translator Philip Stewart the controversial novel *Awlad Haritna* ('Children of our Alley'). He wished to find a work that he could translate for, I think, an MA degree at Oxford; I told him that if he translated the novel I would include it in the Arab Authors series, where it was published under the title *The Children of Gebelawi*. Little did I realize that the novel I had recommended for translation would later become, like Salman Rushdie's *Satanic Verses*, the subject of so much uproar and an attempt on the life of the author. Previously, when the novel was being serialized in *al-Ahram*, pressure was put on the newspaper to stop printing the rest of the book, which the religious authorities claimed was blasphemous. At the same time, the writer himself was being asked by the authorities to explain what the book was about and who the various characters inhabiting the alley in fact represented. I happened to be on one of my periodical visits to Cairo at the time and was told by Naguib Mahfouz of the predicament in which he found himself. I said that he should stick to his guns, state that it is not up to the author to start explaining his work, and refuse to answer any question that might jeopardize him with the religious authorities at al-Azhar. However, it became common knowledge that *al-Ahram* had stopped publication of the novel, and the book was no longer available in Egypt (though an edition, printed in Beirut, could always be bought at one of the better bookshops in downtown Cairo). The English translation was also banned in Egypt and the matter culminated in 1994 (more than thirty years after the book had been serialized in *al-Ahram*), when an extreme Islamist, believing the book to be blasphemous (though it was said he had never read it), attacked the writer and badly wounded him by stabbing him in the neck.

When, following the award of the Nobel prize to Mahfouz, it was decided to produce a uniform edition of most of his work, Philip Stewart was invited to have his translation included among the official translations being produced by the AUC Press and Doubleday in America, but, having seen that other translators of the book had been subject to attack, he decided to allow some other translator to make a new official rendering of this contentious novel into English. I was offered the job, but declined, and it was then offered to the American translator Peter Theroux, brother of the well-known travel writer Paul Theroux. His translation was published under the title *Children of the Alley* in New York in 1996, and with the AUC Press's twenty-volume anniversary edition at the author's ninetieth birthday in 2001.

6

While I was still with the BBC's Arabic Service I had read some of Yahya Hakki's writing, so once I was in Cairo he was one of the writers I made contact with. I must confess that at that time I found Yahya Hakki a difficult writer, one much preoccupied with the finer points of language. Soon after arriving in Cairo I translated and published locally a short story of his entitled "Story in the Form of a Petition." I then translated the story "Mother of the Destitute," the original of which, as far as I remember, was first published in the magazine *al-Katib al-misri*, edited by Taha Hussein, and it was this story that I selected to represent Yahya Hakki in my first volume of Arabic short stories. Later on I remember him suggesting that I translate a story of his called "The Spiral Staircase." It deals with the back staircase to a large building of flats and the servants employed in the flats and the various tradesmen who toiled up and down this staircase on their diverse errands. It was a fairly long story, and his rich combination of the classical and colloquial languages posed a number of difficulties for me. We spent, I recollect, many an hour together going through my translation, and somewhere in all my papers—lying in the drawer of a desk or in an old suitcase (I would not have thrown it away)—is my unpublished translation of that story, with his copious explanations and suggestions. In vain I tried to locate it when the AUC Press asked me to produce a book of stories by Yahya Hakki.

Of all the writers I got to know in Cairo during those early years, Yahya Hakki was one of the few who became a truly personal friend. We would meet up in various cafes and would sometimes lunch together. He was a person, older than myself, whom I felt I could rely on if, as a foreigner, I should ever need help. This in fact happened, as I have related in an earlier chapter. I left Cairo in 1949, and around the same time it seems Yahya was appointed to the Egyptian Embassy in Paris, for while I was in Tehran, often feeling nostalgic for the familiar Cairo, I received a letter from him on embassy paper. It was full of the warmth and gentle sense of humor that were characteristic of him, written in a lighthearted mixture of the classical and colloquial languages. Disorganized in my life generally, I don't as a rule keep letters, though I am pleased that I am still in possession of this one.

To Yahya I confided my ambition to produce a volume of Arabic short stories taken from all over the Arab world and to find a publisher for it in Britain. It would be the first publication to attempt to introduce modern Arabic literature to the west. In the following years I lived for the most part outside Egypt but would visit Cairo on a regular basis. On each occasion Yahya and I would meet up and he would inquire, with a twisted smile, how my volume of Arabic short stories was faring. Both of us secretly knew that the project was perhaps so much pie in the sky and would never be realized. Even if I found the necessary material, how would I find a publisher for so outlandish a book? But the day came when the volume was finished, and good fortune produced a friend in London who 'knew somebody who knew somebody' who worked with Oxford University Press. This meant that at least the book would be seriously considered. In the end the volume of stories was accepted for publication as a work of scholarship rather than for any literary merits it might have; there was also one condition: that a scholar of distinction should write an introduction to it. While I was known to Professor Arberry, who at that time held the Chair of Arabic at Cambridge—I had once mislaid a talk of his when I was at the BBC Arabic Service—I happened to know that he did not regard me as a serious person. I nevertheless wrote to him asking if he would be so good as to write the necessary introduction. This he agreed to do, despite the fact that he was by then a sick man, and also that the modern literary movement was not a subject about which he was particularly knowledgeable. But, then, who was at that time?

And so, on my next visit to Cairo, I was able to tell Yahya that a volume entitled *Modern Arabic Short Stories* would be coming out from no less a publisher than Oxford University Press. It was produced with an unusual cover designed by a friend of mine, the Sudanese artist Ibrahim al-Salahi, made up of the names of the writers contained in the volume written in Arabic calligraphy and forming the shape of a horse. The year was 1967, however—not the best year in which to produce a volume of Arabic short stories, and several English publications refused to review the book. The situation was not helped by the fact that no Arab government or institution bought a single copy of the book, and Oxford University Press were unable to sell the very limited edition they had printed; it was later sold off as a paperback in Lebanon. Only recently I saw that Oxford had produced a volume of Japanese short stories, so I wrote to them and suggested that, having produced the first ever volume of stories translated from the Arabic, they should, after this long lapse of time, be the publishers to produce a further, up-to-date volume. They answered that volumes of short stories were difficult to sell—it would seem, particularly Arabic ones!

The Oxford volume enjoyed a new lease of life when it was reissued as a paperback in the Arab Authors series, which I started at the invitation of James Currey of Heinemann. James was the editor of the still popular African Writers series. I had been able to include in this series books by a number of Arab writers who happened to be African, writers such as Naguib Mahfouz, Tewfik al-Hakim, and Tayeb Salih. What, though, I asked James, about writers from say Palestine or Iraq? And so it was agreed, provided I acted as a consultant to the series (there being no one at Heinemann who had any idea about modern Arabic literature), that a new Arab Authors series should be started. This series devoted exclusively to translations from Arabic continued for several years and published some twenty-four titles. The series played a vital role, I believe, in introducing the best products of the Arab literary renaissance to the English-reading public; at the same time, the titles were also taken up in the United States by Three Continents Press.

In the late 1980s, James Currey and Keith Sambrook, both directors of Heinemann Educational, confided in me that there had been a take-over of Heinemann, and that the new auditors had found that the Arab Authors series was not showing a profit. It should be explained that the African Writers series had the advantage of publishing in the main books written originally in English and therefore had markets in those African countries where English was known. The Arab Authors, on the other hand, published solely books translated from Arabic and therefore had no market in the Arab world. So I was informed that the series I had started would be closed down—this happened literally months before Naguib Mahfouz was awarded the Nobel prize—unless some sort of financial help could be found from the Arab world. What sort of amount did they have in mind? Well, a mere, say, £5,000 would help. And yet the sad thing was that I was unable to find even this small amount of support for the series from any source in the Arab world.

In the end, the titles from the Arab Authors series were sold in the 1980s to the AUC Press. I was naturally unhappy that the series I had spent so much time building up, and over which I had had virtual control, should be discontinued, but at least some of the titles still feature in the AUC Press catalog, and new translations from modern Arabic literature are regularly being brought out.

I always regretted not having translated more of Yahya Hakki's work, and I was thus happy to take up the suggestion of the AUC Press to put together a small volume of his work, the main part of which would consist of his novella *The Lamp of Umm Hashim*—this volume appeared in 2004.

The last time I saw Yahya Hakki was when he was invited to the American University in Cairo in 1987. He was somewhat frail, and came with his wife. He didn't give a lecture but proposed to answer questions from the audience, which we were asked to write down on pieces of paper; these were then handed to someone who read out the question to Yahya Hakki. I asked why it was that while Egyptians were well known for their sense of humor, there seemed to be so little humor in the writings of Egyptian authors. I was unaware at that time that he had himself posed this question in one of his essays, and had found no adequate answer. Another member of the audience asked whether he had ever thought that he might one day win the Nobel prize. He made as though to consider the question for a few seconds, after which, with that enigmatic smile of his, he replied that, No, he had never entertained such a dream, knowing as he did that somewhere else in Cairo there was another writer, more talented and more industrious than himself who was laboring away. Nevertheless, late in life he was awarded the King Faisal Prize for his services to Arabic literature, though his state of health did not permit him to travel to Saudi Arabia to receive it. In the meantime he had typically refused the Saddam Hussein Prize.

Then, one day in 1992, as I was making my way out to my home in Fayoum, I heard on the radio of the death of Yahya Hakki, at the age of 87. Some people seem to be able to attend funerals of their friends without being too affected. I am not such a person, so I continued on my way. However, each time I go out to Cairo airport—and it is several times a year—I pass by al-Ghazali Street in Heliopolis and am reminded of going to lunch at his flat there with him and his French wife.

7

Louis Awad was one of the most versatile intellectuals of his time. Though several years my senior, we had overlapped at Cambridge. Coming from a very modest background—am I right in saying that his father was a station master in some remote part of the country?—Louis, living at a time when talented students were sent on scholarships to Europe, took a doctorate in English literature at Cambridge. So when I turned up in Cairo in 1945 as a teacher of Arabic translation at the British Institute, I immediately made contact with him. I enjoyed his company, and we would often meet at Groppi's or at a new cafe called Marly (now extinct), where Louis would sit by the hour doing the various translations commissioned by the powerful and imaginative literary publishing house, al-Katib al-Misri, headed by Taha Hussein; it also produced a monthly magazine entitled *al-Katib al-misri*, which carried regular articles by Louis on modern literary figures such writers as T.S. Eliot. I remember, for instance, his excellent translation of the poem "The Hollow Men." He also wrote articles on William Faulkner and Samuel Beckett. Among the books he translated were Oscar Wilde's *The Picture of Dorian Gray*. He was a first-class translator, having of course an excellent knowledge of both English and Arabic. All his writings were done in a meticulous hand that had the precision of hieroglyphics rather than the naturally cursive style of Arabic.

During my early time in Cairo, Louis gave me the manuscript of his novel *The Phoenix, or the History of Hasan Muftah* to read. He first wrote the novel in colloquial Arabic, then decided to render it into the classical language, and this was the version that he eventually published in 1966 in Beirut. In the introduction he gives the names of five people who had read the novel in manuscript during the late 1940s, mine among them. He also mentions that, years later, in 1965 it was read by none less than Tewfik al-Hakim and Hussein Fawzi, both of whom were employed with Louis at *al-Ahram*. It seems that Tewfik al-Hakim had remarked that had the novel been published when it was written in the 1940s, it would have changed the course of the Arabic novel. Hussein Fawzi was also very enthusiastic about it. Louis mentions in the introduction that I had expressed the wish to translate the novel, and that he had asked me to hold back until the Arabic edition had appeared. The reason he had not published it earlier was that King Farouk was still on the throne, and the novel would certainly have been banned, as had happened to *The Sufferers* by no less a figure than Taha Hussein. An odd, disturbing piece of writing, *Hasan Muftah* had a Dostoyevskian air of gloom about it in which was mingled a dark element of the fantastic. Years later, I published a chapter from it in the magazine *Aswat*, which I had started in London in the early 1960s. The novel seems to have attracted very little notice at the time it came out, and it is now unavailable. If not a success as a novel, it was certainly an unusual piece of writing, especially for its time. I even translated a part of it, but it presented a formidable task that I was certainly not prepared to undertake without a guaranteed publisher. Has Louis's novel, then, sunk without trace?

Louis's interest in the colloquial language is shown by his experiment in writing an autobiographical book about his student days in England in colloquial Egyptian Arabic *(Mudhakkarat talib bi'tha)*, as well as a volume of poetry.

Through Louis I met a number of interesting characters in Cairo. A common threesome was made up of Louis, Ibrahim Shukrallah, and myself. Ibrahim was employed for a time by the Press Office of the British Council, after which he left to make a career for himself in the Arab League. He had an excellent command of English and had collaborated with a certain Herbert Howarth on producing an anthology of translations from Arabic literature that was quite novel in its approach to translation, certainly where Arabic was concerned, where strictly academic renderings were all that were available. The book was entitled *Images from the Arab World* and was recently republished in paperback by Gazelle Publications. It contained translations from the very earliest pre-Islamic poets, right up to examples of *zagal*, the form of poetry written in the colloquial language and of which Bairam al-Tunsi was at that time the leading exponent; it also included extracts from some of the most interesting but least known works of prose. I assume that the selections were culled by Ibrahim from his extensive readings in Arabic.

Ibrahim Shukrallah was primarily a press man and a journalist, but he was also creatively talented. He wrote several short stories, some of which I translated, and one of which, "The Mother," I published in the Beirut magazine *Middle East Forum*, edited by Rosemary Sayegh, the English wife of the economist Professor Yusuf Sayegh and sister-in-law of my friend the poet Tawfic Sayegh. I tried to persuade Ibrahim to write more stories, as those few he had passed on to me in manuscript form were superior to most of the fiction that was being written at the time, but he did not seem to have the will. Many years later, not so long before he died, he suddenly produced a volume of Arabic poetry that was very well received by those who could recognize original work when they saw it.

Ibrahim had a distinguished career in the Arab League. Was it he who introduced me to the then Secretary General of the Arab League, Abdel Rahman Azzam, who wrote the introduction to my small volume of short stories by Mahmoud Teymour? Certainly Ibrahim wrote a review of the book in *The Egyptian Gazette*, at that time in effect the only English-language publication in Egypt. He later served in India and elsewhere and then headed the Arab League Office in London, where we would meet up periodically.

One affectionate memory I have of Ibrahim Shukrallah was during the worst night of riots against the British, in late 1946, I think. I was living in a small flat alongside a large building not far from what was then Midan Soliman Pasha. The entrance to the flat was by a long iron stairway that ran up the side of the building. On the day of the riots I found myself imprisoned in the room, as crowds passed by in the street below shouting death to the English and breaking any shop windows that hadn't been shuttered. On several occasions individuals would climb up the iron stairway and bang on my door. I stayed on inside, quiet as a mouse. As my flat consisted of no more than a bedroom, a shower, and a lavatory, I had no food. Thus by the end of the day, I was feeling hungry. However, the mood out on the streets was not encouraging, and I remained inside my room, determined if it came to it to go supperless to bed. As night began to fall, I could hear more steps coming up the stairway. My name was called out as someone banged on my door, and I recognized Ibrahim's voice. I let him in and told him that I was in need of nothing but a good meal. So we went out to a kebab restaurant we used to frequent, and I remember, as I entered with certain misgivings, the people turning round and smiling at this obvious Englishman who had dared to put his head into the lion's mouth.

Besides introducing me to a number of Cairo's leading intellectuals, Louis Awad would accompany me to Taha Hussein's weekly soiree, which was attended by many of the leading professors and lecturers at Cairo University and the main contributors to the monthly magazine he edited. I was always amused that Louis, who cared not at all for his personal appearance and somehow managed to have a permanent three-day growth of beard, always insisted on going to a barber's for a shave on those evenings when we went to see Taha Hussein, Egypt's most famous blind man. Taha Hussein was very much the center of the salon, and much of the conversation was often in French when foreigners were present. It says much for Egypt at the time that someone like Taha Hussein, blind at a very young age and from a lowly background, could achieve university education at the Sorbonne and then achieve the rank of Minister of Culture.

Among Louis's numerous publications was his book of poetry in the colloquial language, which he published under the title *Plutoland*. It was a volume influenced by his wide reading of English poetry; it broke new ground and is still read by a discerning few. The book, as it happens, owed its existence partly to me as, shortly before taking off for the summer to Paris, Louis told me he had no money and borrowed twenty Egyptian pounds from me with which to have the book printed. Today twenty pounds wouldn't buy you much of a meal but in those days—and for such as myself and Louis—it was a considerable sum. I recollect protesting heatedly with Louis on his return from Paris, where he had spent the summer and, to boot, had acquired a wife, that I had been forced to remain on in the heat of the summer, whereas he had somehow found the funds for a trip to Paris, so would he please return the twenty pounds he'd borrowed!

Louis was a man of courage and principle. His Communist leanings led to him being imprisoned in the days of Nasser, and while I don't think he was at all religious, he was proud of his Coptic background, proud too of being Egyptian. It is said that while he was in prison, his sole request was for a grammar of the Coptic language. He had, incidentally, taught himself both Latin and Greek, besides having an excellent command of English and French. He was well known for his shabby appearance and his disregard for the material things of life—apart from books. A joke went the rounds that someone was proudly showing a friend around a flat he had just acquired. Showing him the lounge, he described it as being furnished it in the style of Louis Seize. Then, on opening up a higgledy-piggledy box-room, he declared it a la Louis Awad!

I returned to live in Cairo in 1974 after a four-year period spent in Beirut, and Louis and I continued to be in touch. By this time his interests had become scholarly rather than literary, and he had little time for the creative work that was being produced. Then came the day when I was informed that Louis was seriously ill in hospital. I visited him and was asked by the nurse if I could possibly persuade him to stop his addictive smoking. It was a futile request and had come far too late. In a matter of a few weeks Louis Awad was dead.

8

A major writer who has long been a friend is Edwar al-Kharrat. One of his stories was included in the Oxford University Press book of *Modern Arabic Short Stories*. It was from his first volume, *High Walls*. Since then he has produced a further five collections of stories and no less than fourteen novels. My last volume of Arabic short stories, published in 2000 by the American University in Cairo Press, also contained a story by him, though I was hard put to it to find one that did not present insuperable difficulties both for myself as translator and for the reader. He continues to grow more recondite in his writings and risks becoming a 'writer's writer,' though two novels about Alexandria, translated by Frances Liardet, can be read with real enjoyment. Ferial Ghazoul and John Verlenden of the American University in Cairo have undertaken, not without considerable difficulty at their own admission, an excellent rendering into English of Edwar's novel *Rama and the Dragon*.

Edwar has all along been a great encourager of younger talents, many of which were first introduced to a wider public through the magazine *Gallery 67*, which he edited. These include such writers as Ibrahim Aslan, Mohamed El-Bisatie, and the late Yahya Taher Abdullah. His small flat in Zamalek—made small by the abundance of books—where I first met him in the 1940s, is a regular meeting-place for budding writers. One evening—I recollect that Mustafa Badawi, who taught Arabic at Oxford University, was in Cairo on a visit—a number of younger writers were present. That evening it was brought home to me how the translator from a language such as Arabic differs from one who translates from say French or German. The latter relies upon publishers to choose the books they wish to have translated. Would the translator be interested in such-and-such a novel? What sort of fee would he or she require? This approach of course doesn't operate where Arabic is concerned. There is no publishing house in London employing anyone interested in modern Arabic literature or capable of reading Arabic. As an Arabic translator, therefore, having read a book that I feel deserves to be translated, I can either sit down and translate the work in question in the hope that, when the time comes, I will find a publisher for it, or I must have at my disposal a publisher who has sufficient confidence in my judgment and will publish anything I care to translate—as happened with the Heinemann Arab Authors series. I know that many Arab writers—and Tayeb Salih has expressed this opinion to me openly—feel that attempts should have been made to find mainstream publishers for Arabic works of fiction. In the case of Tayeb himself, I was grateful to have the Arab Authors series at my disposal, otherwise his novel *Season of Migration to the North* might well have remained unpublished. At least, through its own merits, the novel later achieved translation into a number of languages beside English, and has even now found its way into the prestigious Penguin Modern Classics. As a translator's main concern is to be assured that his efforts are going to be rewarded by seeing the book in print, I have always sought to find a publisher who could be relied upon to look favorably on translations from the Arabic. However, it required Naguib Mahfouz to win the Nobel prize for an American publisher of the caliber of Doubleday to take him on. Today publishers are primarily businesspeople and are loath to take risks, particularly with a book translated from Arabic. English readers, it is known, keep away from any translated book, be it even from French. Consider, for example, the work of the Lebanese writer Amin Maalouf, who writes in French. The rights to a novel of his that had sold over a million copies in France were bought by Quartet Books in London, and the resulting English edition sold a mere two thousand copies. Arabic translators thus, in many ways, have both greater power and more responsibility than their French counterparts, for they take upon themselves not only the role of translator but also that of the person deciding what should be translated. By choosing to translate X, you are seen as rejecting both Y and Z (who may well be just as good, or even better than X.)

That the role of the Arabic translator is both difficult and unenviable was brought home to me that evening that I spent at Edwar al-Kharrat's flat with several of Cairo's younger writers, one of whom suddenly demanded of me: "Who are you to choose what writers you translate?" I was taken aback by the question and was grateful to Edwar when he intervened and asked the young man: "So what do you want him to do if not to make the choice himself?" The young man answered: "He should go to the Ministry of Culture and get a list of the books that should be translated." This reply evinced general merriment, for it is well known that the establishment has its own favorites, and these are not necessarily the best. Edwar continued by pointing out that in the end it was I who was going to have all the work of translating the book, so why should I translate a book that might not be to my liking? Also, being English, was I not better qualified to judge which book would be likely to be well received by the English reader? I was grateful to Edwar for answering for me, aware as I am of the feeling that must inevitably exist among many writers who have not had their work translated for one reason or another. It is a sad fact that it is only by being translated that the Arab writer has a chance of achieving any serious recognition and at least the possibility of some real monetary reward. It should also be borne in mind that translating Arabic fiction is poorly rewarded in financial terms—if one practiced translation in order to supplement one's income, one would be better off using one's time giving private English lessons. This is not something that is generally appreciated. Thus my friend Said al-Kafrawi, when I produced a volume of his short stories in English translation and the publisher's contract stipulated that we were to share the royalties fifty/fifty, was astonished to find that his share was a mere pittance. "But haven't you been making a living out of translation all these years?" he asked me. The short answer was: "No—thank God!"

Today the lot of the writer in Egypt, for instance, is dire. The money he or she can make from a book would not pay for the typing of it, and even established writers are now actually paying publishers to have their work appear in print. So what are the joys of being a writer in the Arab world other than the prestige that may go with it? Because of the present situation for the writer, the attractions of being translated become greater: even if, for instance, being translated doesn't put much money in the pocket, it does at least open the door to being invited to various conferences in, say, Tunisia or Morocco, or, if the writer is lucky, to spend several days in France or some other European country with all expenses paid and who knows what other doors opening up. I was not altogether surprised when one evening I had a phone call from a well-known writer whose work had as yet to appear in translation. He proposed that I should translate one of his novels and that he would pay me any reasonable fee I liked to suggest; he would also sign away all the rights in the book to me. I told him that I did not translate primarily for money, but that one day, God willing, I would translate one of his books. He has now, I am glad to say, several books in English translation.

The only other publication apart from the slim volume of short stories by Teymour that I produced during my time in Cairo during the 1940s was a small book entitled *Passages for Translation, from and into Arabic*. At the time I was giving translation lessons at the British Institute and found myself continually faced at the last moment with choosing and producing specimen pieces for translation, run off on the roneo for the students. The Anglo-Egyptian Bookshop, which sometimes ventured into the realm of publishing, agreed to publish the book. The owner of the bookshop was Sobhi Grais; during the years between 1949 when I left Cairo and my return in 1974, I would make a point of calling on Sobhi whenever I was in town. He was by then long past the age at which people generally retire, but Sobhi continued to be in charge of the bookshop until he was well into his nineties. During these years, each time we met, he would inquire with real concern about my mother, who had come out to Cairo in the late 1940s and much enjoyed her life there, staying on for a time even when I had left. She had long ago passed away, but on each occasion I saw Sobhi he would ask after my mother and I would have to explain that she had, sadly, passed away. The scene would be repeated year after year until he himself also passed away.

One of my students, Mohamed Habib, who had become a friend, would sometimes of an evening help me out with the notes to the English-to-Arabic passages. He was an ex-sailor and had been on the king's yacht *al-Mahrusa*. He had written a description of his time on the boat, including his brutal flogging, and he had asked me to keep this manuscript for him in case—being a member of the Muslim Brotherhood—his room was searched. Then, one evening, he suddenly asked me—whom he had taken on several occasions to meet Hassan al-Banna, the head of the Brotherhood, and whom he had asked to keep in his possession a highly dangerous manuscript—a quite simple and direct question: was I a British spy? Of course, in a way, his question was understandable: why wasn't I living, like every other respectable Englishman, in great style in a flat in Zamalek and going regularly to the British Club? I merely mention this because this is the natural suspicion one is bound to arouse by deciding to take on someone else's country. Fifty years later an Egyptian academic wrote a piece in *al-Ahram*—to whose English-language weekly edition I am a regular contributor—saying that while in Cairo during the war I was a British spy, and that during that time I had succeeded in 'picking up' a bit of Arabic. The fact that I hadn't happened to be in Cairo during the war at all was irrelevant. Many friends expressed their sorrow and apologies, while all I could do was tell myself that this was the price one paid for trying to put down roots in a foreign field.

9

When Naguib Mahfouz was awarded the Nobel prize for literature in 1988, I suggested to the American University in Cairo Press that they should set up an annual prize under his name for the best novel in Arabic. For some years nothing was done about this until Mark Linz, who had been the director of the Press for three years in the mid-1980s, returned to Cairo in 1995 to take up the same post. I put the idea to him and he was enthusiastic about it. He decided that the prize, the Naguib Mahfouz Medal for Literature, would consist of a silver medal plus one thousand dollars, and would also include the novel being translated into English and being published by the AUC Press. He and I paid a visit to Naguib Mahfouz, who welcomed the idea and expressed the wish that I should be on the committee that would be set up to choose the winning novel. Later, however, thinking the matter over, I decided to withdraw, as I felt that the committee should be composed solely of Egyptians, or at least Arabs. The prize was first awarded in 1996, and since then it has achieved a certain eminence: the quality of the translations has been good and the standard of the production and marketing of the finished product as professional as any books published in the west. Even so, only one of the prize-winning novels in translation has found a separate publisher in London or New York, and so the AUC Press established its own sales agreements there to distribute the book directly in Europe and North America.

While I was the first person to translate Naguib Mahfouz—a story from his very first volume—I later translated a much more mature story by him entitled "Zaabalawi," which I included in the Oxford University Press volume of *Modern Arabic Short Stories* and which then found its way into the Norton anthology, *Masterpieces of World Literature*, where it is the only example of writing from modern Arabic literature. Before he was awarded the Nobel prize I had not translated a complete book by Mahfouz, but after the prize and once the AUC Press had entered into a contract with Doubleday to jointly publish the greater part of his work in English translation, I was given the opportunity to translate some of his work, on favorable terms. I chose first of all to produce a selection of his short stories, feeling that such a volume should do reasonably well and that, along the years, stories would be taken from it for publication in anthologies. This has in fact proved to be the case, and the short story "Zaabalawi" has been republished several times, particularly in the United States.

While translating one of the stories for the volume, I experienced a difficulty often encountered by translators of Arabic, namely misprints and other errors. In "The Conjuror Made Off with the Dish," I came to the final paragraph and could make nothing of it; I consulted an Egyptian friend well read in Mahfouz's work, but he was unable to help. I therefore rang up the writer himself, who admitted that something was sadly wrong with the text and solved the difficulty by providing a whole line that had been omitted by the printers. No one, it seems, had noticed that a vital piece of the story was missing! Such errors occur because Arabic publishers in Egypt do not trouble to employ editors to go through material they are printing. Also, quite apart from making sure that errors do not creep into the printed text, an editor may suggest to the writer that certain changes should be made. I know of several Arabic novels that would have greatly benefited from having an editor tactfully suggest to the author that cuts could usefully be made.

After completing the representative volume of short stories by Naguib Mahfouz, I then chose to translate a short novel of his entitled *The Journey of Ibn Fattouma*, a sort of Egyptian *Pilgrim's Progress*. The basic idea was a good one, but I felt the author never really developed sufficient enthusiasm for the theme of the novel. While translating it I found that the hero's name suddenly changed in the middle of the book. I rang the author up about this, and he was greatly amused at my discovery. "So which name shall I call him?" I asked. "Choose whichever you like best," he replied with a laugh. It is such inconsistencies and misprints that show that Arabic publishing is in need of editors.

With the English translations being well produced by Doubleday in conjunction with the AUC Press, I felt encouraged to take on a further novel by Naguib Mahfouz. This time I chose a longer one with the Arabic title *Nights of a Thousand Nights*, recommended to me by my friend the writer Abdou Gubeir. I felt it read well in English and decided that the title *Arabian Nights and Days* had more relevance to the English-language reader already familiar with *The Arabian Nights*: another instance, in my opinion, where strict adherence to the original would have served little purpose. While I am scrupulous in translation about neither adding anything to the original nor omitting anything—however tempted I may be!—one cannot but be aware that English and Arabic are very different languages and, in the end, one is seeking to provide a rendering that is both comprehensible and pleasurable to the reader of English. *Arabian Nights and Days* sold reasonably well and was short-listed in England for the *Independent* Prize for works of fiction in translation. And now, several years later, I have read in the Arabic literary weekly, *Akhbar al-adab*, that a limited edition of the book, with specially done illustrations, has been produced in the United States.

Finally, I chose to translate a volume of Mahfouz's personal reflections, *Echoes of an Autobiography*. This then came out with an introduction by Nadine Gordimer, another Nobel prize winner and an admirer of Mahfouz's writings.

Before leaving the subject of the only Arab writer to receive the Nobel prize, it is interesting to note that some years before Mahfouz was awarded the prize, an English writer of distinction, John Fowles, had read Mahfouz's novel *Miramar* in translation and had written a very perceptive and appreciative introduction to it. This translation, together with the introduction, appeared in Heinemann's Arab Authors series. After Mahfouz had won the prize, *Miramar* continued to be published in an edition produced by the AUC Press and Doubleday, but without Fowles' introduction. Why? The reason no doubt was that the introduction had ended with a long quotation from Naguib Mahfouz in which he modestly expressed the opinion that he was ranked among the third rather than the first rank of writers. This to my mind doesn't necessarily place him among the third rank but simply shows what a modest person he is. In any case, John Fowles himself is a considerable talent and it is surely of interest to find such a writer praising Mahfouz at a time before he had obtained the endorsement of the Nobel prize. It is now conveniently forgotten that at one time many of the habitués of Cairo's Café Riche were labeling Mahfouz as 'old hat.'

10

To continue as a lecturer at Cairo University seemed to me to be an ideal way of life—while one was not overpaid, one was also not overworked. But my father had been ill and I had not visited England since leaving in 1945, so I decided to go back to London in the summer of 1949. I certainly had no intention of seeking another job, but it happened that I met someone in London who offered me a position as Middle East representative of a company that printed banknotes. After a year spent in Iran on their behalf I did a tour of the Middle East; this included a visit to Baghdad. As it happened, Baghdad had become the home of my Palestinian friend Jabra Ibrahim Jabra, whom I had first got to know when we overlapped for a while at Cambridge.

While the Iraqi government was not interested in printing new notes with the company I was representing, I decided nonetheless to stay on in Baghdad in order to spend time with Jabra and the interesting friends who had collected round him, many of them, like him, teaching at Baghdad University. I moved into the cheapest hotel I could find—a move that alerted the Baghdad police—and spent my days and half my nights with the literary coterie of Iraq's capital. It was only many years later that a Palestinian writer friend in Abu Dhabi told me that he had read about me in Jabra's autobiography. In it, Jabra describes my stay in Baghdad, including the joke he and I had played on Boland al-Haydari, later to become one of the leading poets in the new movement of poetry in the Arab world. Boland was intrigued to meet an Englishman who spoke Arabic, and he and I spent many hours talking about the poetry of T.S. Eliot, Dylan Thomas, etc. At that time the existentialist movement was a popular topic of discussion among Arab intellectuals, and Boland, despite having no knowledge of any foreign language, was particularly interested in it. Jabra and I hatched a plot by pretending to Boland that Sartre had suddenly been inspired to break into verse and to compose his one and only poem, which happened to be about existentialism. This poem, we explained, had been translated from the French into English and published in a British literary magazine, of which I had brought a copy with me; Jabra and I had then sat down and translated the poem into Arabic to show to Boland, in the hope that he might, with his knowledge of existentialism, be able to solve one or two obscurities. Together, Jabra and I composed a poem in Arabic in which we laid various traps for our unsuspecting friend. I remember that I myself contributed a reference to 'the stranger' so that Boland might later explain to us that this of course referred to Camus's novel of that title. It was a cruel hoax, but it was taken in good part by Boland, whom I was later to meet on various occasions in Beirut and once at the airport in Cairo, as well as on and off in London, where he settled with his wife. It was a shock to learn of his death in 1996: on one of my periodical visits to London, I rang his home and his wife answered the phone. After the usual pleasantries, I asked to speak to Boland, only to be told that he had just died. Boland is now recognized as one of the leading poets in the modern movement and has been honored by having a poetry prize in his name presented at the yearly literary festival that takes place in the summer at the Moroccan coastal town of Asilah, to the south of Tangier.

During my various trips to Baghdad I would generally stay with Jabra and his Iraqi wife Lamia. A naturally gifted person, Jabra came from a lowly background and had been born in Bethlehem. He had been sent by the British, who ruled Palestine at that time, on a scholarship to

Cambridge, where he took a degree in English literature. His creative gifts extended to poetry (of which he had volumes published in both English and Arabic), the novel, and the short story, as well as literary criticism. In addition, he was an art critic and wrote extensively about the exceptionally talented body of artists in Baghdad at that time. His translations into Arabic extended to some half dozen of Shakespeare's plays, and, *inter alia*, Faulkner's novel, *The Sound and the Fury*. He also made the interesting experiment of rendering Beckett's *Waiting for Godot* into the colloquial Iraqi dialect. His home in the Mansour district of Baghdad might equally as well have been in Oxford, or perhaps Paris: books covered those parts of the walls that weren't occupied by reproductions of paintings by such artists as Chagall, or by the paintings or drawings of Jabra's artist friends, or by his own paintings. No wonder he was disconcerted when someone told him that, for his own health and well-being, he should give place of honor on his walls to a portrait of the country's beloved president. In later years, when I had started up the quarterly literary magazine *Aswat* in London, he contributed a long article with illustrations about Iraq's leading artist Jawad Selim, who was to die at an early age from a heart attack. Many years later, on a brief visit to Paris, I was given by the Iraqi writer and journalist Inaam Kachachi a book she had written about Lorna, Jawad Selim's English widow.

At one time, during the 1950s and 60s, Jabra would pay frequent visits to London, generally for the purpose of supervising the recording of commentaries to documentary films made by the Iraqi Petroleum Company, for which he was then working as press officer. Often during these visits he and I would get together with the poet Tawfic Sayegh, who was then a lecturer at the School of Oriental and African Studies. Tawfic, too, was a regular contributor to *Aswat*, and contributed a translation of Eliot's "Four Quartets." *Aswat*, a quarterly magazine that lasted only twelve issues, gave me the opportunity of introducing in Arabic many of my favorite writings. Each issue included a short story, sometimes by such Arab writers as Ghassan Kanafani and Zakaria Tamer, at others with stories translated from the English, such as a story by Joyce from *The Dubliners*, a little known story by Dylan Thomas, and one by Isak

Dinesen. Each issue also included an article, with illustrations, about an artist: Picasso, Hokusai, and one of my favorites, Henri Rousseau. I remember, too, including selections from that strange and favorite work of mine, *The Unquiet Grave* by Palinurus (Cyril Connolly).

As a result of the magazine *Aswat*, I was visited during the early 1960s by a representative from the office of the Congress of Cultural Freedom named John Hunt. An American, he was working in the Paris office of the Congress. He told me that the Congress, which already financed the magazine *Encounter* and its counterparts in French *(Preuves)* and in German *(Der Monat)*, was thinking of publishing a cultural magazine in Arabic, and did I happen to know anyone who would be a suitable editor? There was some suggestion that Yusuf al-Khal from Beirut, already well known as the founder of the magazine *Shi'r* ('Poetry') and the general literary magazine *Adab*, and the owner of an art gallery, would be a suitable choice. I, though, felt that Tawfic would make an excellent editor for such a magazine and would also enjoy the experience, rather than continue teaching Arabic at the School of Oriental and African Studies. I asked Tawfic what he felt about it, and he said he would be interested but only if he were given a completely free hand. I told him it was up to him to lay down his conditions.

I knew Tawfic to be a difficult person, and knew that he would certainly not agree to anything but complete editorial freedom. I myself had had a contretemps with him over a review he had written for *Aswat* about a book on the subject of perfume that I had assigned to him, knowing that it was a book he would like to possess. When he delivered the review I saw that it contained a reference to "the perfume of the underarm" and the poetry of Baudelaire. Thinking that some of my readers might find this objectionable, I deleted the reference, not feeling that I had done anything particularly heinous. However, Tawfic was incensed at what I had done and for a time refused to speak to me. The predicament was eventually settled when Yusuf al-Khal, on a visit to London, insisted that we 'kiss and make up.'

Tawfic was also upset that, not being particularly interested in poetry, I hadn't read any of his own volumes, so I promised that the next book he brought out I would read from cover to cover. When he gave me a copy of his next book, I took it away, and commented when I next met him that I hadn't known he had a child. He was amazed that no one else had spotted the somewhat cryptic reference to his having a daughter, who happened to be by his girlfriend Kay, after whom the volume of poetry *Qasidat Kaf* was named.

An interest that Tawfic and I shared was erotic literature; it was from him that I learned, for instance, of *The Story of O*. He had a remarkable collection of rare Arabic erotic works, and we had agreed that one day we would work together on producing, in English translation, a selection from the Arabic. When he died in the United States, I had no news of what happened to his library, which perhaps he had left back in Beirut.

I had hoped that I had done my friend a good service by proposing him as the editor of the new magazine, which eventually came out under the title *Hiwar* ('Dialog'). The magazine was well received and contained in one of its first issues the whole of the novel *Season of Migration to the North* by Tayeb Salih. However, many people in the Arab world were not happy about its official sponsor, and I well remember a discussion Jabra and I had with Tawfic about it in my flat in London. While both Jabra and Tawfic had written for *Aswat*, neither Jabra nor I had contributed to *Hiwar*. Tawfic was unhappy about this and asked us why we hadn't done so. We both answered that we unfortunately had doubts about *Hiwar* and that neither of us was in a position to risk writing for a magazine that was regarded by many with suspicion. Finally, we convinced Tawfic, for his own good, to pay a visit to Paris and see John Hunt. This he did, and he was persuaded that everything was above board with *Hiwar*. However, only a few months were to pass before it was announced, with complete disregard for the innocent people who would be hurt, that the Congress of Cultural Freedom was in fact financed by the CIA. One cannot help thinking that the American government possesses more pockets than the CIA from which to give out funds to seemingly innocent organizations like the Congress for Cultural Freedom. However, from past experience, one must recognize that America is ham-fisted in such matters and anyone inveigled in their webs should beware of the possible consequences. The Arabic press of course had a field day and directed its wrath against Tawfic, accusing him of being an American spy, with one paper demanding that he be put on trial. During this time he was living in Beirut, where I visited him and found him in very low spirits. Shortly after this he went to the University of California, Berkeley, where he died of a sudden heart attack.

The story of the Congress of Cultural Freedom was told in a book entitled *Who Paid the Piper*, by Frances Stonor Saunders. John Hunt, of course, features in it, and we are told that he left the organization in 1968 and was awarded a CIA medal for services rendered at a secret ceremony on a houseboat on the Seine, and that he later retired to the south of France. I quote from the book a statement made by John Hunt in July 1997: "There were people in India, in the Lebanon, in Africa—men and women who cast their lot in with the Congress on the strength of representations that I, Mike, and others made—who then found themselves caught in the hurricane. And I know that many of them suffered deeply, and no amount of high strategy, moralizing or discussion will make that fact go away. They put their honor and life on the line, and I haven't forgotten that." It is perhaps significant that John Hunt has chosen to retire in France rather than in the United States.

Jabra and I continued to see each other as and when our various travels permitted. I remember him coming to Cairo on one occasion and telling me how difficult life was becoming in Iraq. His monthly pension, it seemed, had become worth no more than a couple of pounds of coffee and he was living off the royalties from his large number of publications published in Beirut. Though he was Palestinian by birth, Iraq had over the years become Jabra's home; much as he disliked the oppressive atmosphere that had taken over, he had little choice but to stay on there.

I knew from personal experience how uncomfortable one could feel politically in Baghdad when, in the 1970s, I went there with some Arab friends from Beirut. My visa was running out, and my friends wanted to stay on longer so they suggested that I go off to the appropriate office and extend it. "But don't speak a word of Arabic," they warned me. I arrived at the office and found that extending my stay was no easy matter. I was asked whether I'd been to Iraq before, to which I answered that I had first gone there in 1949. The official then insisted on looking up the files. What, he asked, was my family name. I answered, "Johnson-Davies." He glowered at me, "Your family name?" he asked again, loudly. I repeated what I had said. "Can you imagine," he called out in Arabic to his colleagues," I keep asking this donkey of a man for his family name and he gives me two names!" There was general laughter. Once again he repeated his question, pronouncing it word by word as though addressing an idiot with hearing difficulties. I then explained as best I could that my family name happened to be two names. He brought down the files containing all the names beginning with the letter J. While he looked through the pages he kept up a non-stop commentary in Arabic on this 'donkey of a man' who said he'd been in the country more than twenty years ago. When nothing could be found in the J files, he brought down the files for names beginning with D, and the same procedure and the same ribald commentary was repeated, with the same appreciative giggling from his audience. Having failed to find my name under the letter D for the year 1949, he then asked me how it was that I claimed to have visited Iraq in 1949 and yet there was nothing recorded in the files? He made it sound as though I was making a false claim. I endeavored to explain that I was not responsible for keeping the records in the files. Taking on the air of an official suddenly faced with someone who was either a halfwit or a criminal, the man now produced a large form that he asked me to fill out so that he could then decide whether or not to give me an extension to my visa. One look at the form showed me that there was no way I could fill it in. Besides enquiring who my grandfather and other remote relatives were, and where and when they were born, it required me to state what foreign languages I knew and my degree of proficiency in speaking, writing, and reading them. If ever there was a Catch-22 situation, this was it! I turned the form over, consulted my watch, then handed it back to the man. "It doesn't matter," I told him. "There's no point in my staying on longer in Baghdad. I'll leave tomorrow." At this the man relented and gave me an extension to my visa without any filling in of forms.

On one of his visits to Cairo I told Jabra I was giving a short talk about translation, and would he like to attend? He did so and proved a useful member of the audience. The lecture, given at the American University in Cairo, was attended largely by people from the capital's other universities. During the lecture I had given it as my opinion that, on the whole, a translator should confine his activities to translating into his own language. When it came to question time, several people in the audience protested against my suggestion that one should translate only into one's own language, arguing that who could know a language better, he who was born into it or he who had acquired a knowledge of it out of books? I in turn was arguing that if as a translator one was faced by something in the text one wasn't sure about, one could always seek the help of someone whose native language it was, whereas it was surely necessary that one be completely 'at home' with the language into which one was translating. I could see, however, that my arguments were not to the liking of many of my audience and was relieved when Jabra rose to his feet and asked the person chairing the meeting to be allowed to answer the question on my behalf. He then pointed out that he had published poetry and a complete novel in English, and that he had translated several plays by Shakespeare and other writings from English into Arabic, yet it had never occurred to him to translate anything from Arabic into English, not even his own writings. "That," he concluded, "I leave to my good friend Denys." After such a statement it was difficult for anyone to argue against my views on translation.

On Jabra's last visit to Cairo, I went to see him at the hotel. "How are things in Baghdad?" I asked innocently. He looked around at the corners of the room, accustomed as he was to rooms being bugged, and we went out into the open air before he replied to my question. Months later, in Baghdad, Jabra Ibrahim Jabra suffered another heart attack, this time fatal.

Rehearsing a propaganda play, *Qahwat al-hurriya* (Freedom Café) in the BBC Near East Department, Arabic Section, October 1941. Left to right: Shaykh Mohamed Mahmoud Gomaa (the author's teacher at the School of Oriental Studies), Mohamed al-Ghazzawi (producer of plays), Isa Khalil Sabbagh (who became an accredited war correspondent and later worked for Voice of America), Ahmed Taher, the author, Edward Ammoun.

With Jabra Ibrahim Jabra in London, late 1960s.

Tewfik al-Hakim. The dedication on the back of the photograph reads: "To my friend, Denys Johnson-Davies. My picture with the donkeys, and it is not necessary to ask what is meant by the donkeys: that is on the occasion of his translation of The Donkeys' Market into English in his well-known wonderful style." It is signed in English and Arabic and is dated 1973. Photograph by Mohamed Yusuf.

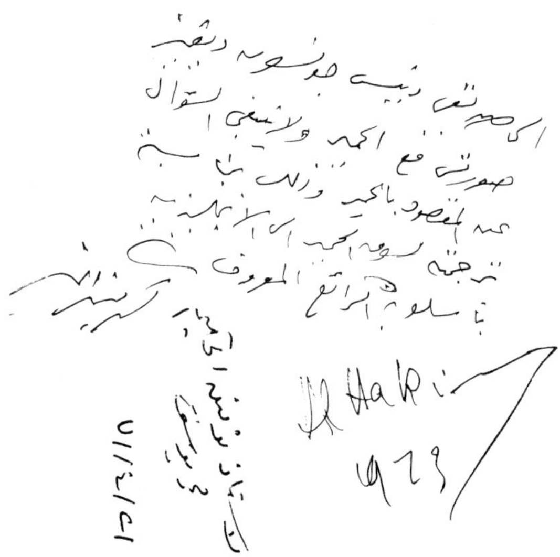

The author in Baghdad, 1949. Photograph by Jabra Ibrahim Jabra.

Boland al-Haidari, Iraqi poet, Baghdad, 1949. Photograph by the author.

With Tawfic Sayigh, Palestinian poet, London, late 1960s. Photograph by Jabra Ibrahim Jabra.

With Egypt's Nobel laureate Naguib Mahfouz, at his home in 1996. Photograph by Paola Crociani.

The author at work at his home in Fayoum, Egypt. Photograph by Paola Crociani.

Yahya Taher Abdullah (left), writer and good friend of the author.

With Abdel Salam al-Ujaili in Aleppo, Syria. Photograph by Paola Crociani.

With Mohamed Barrada, the Moroccan writer and critic, in Cairo. Photograph by Paola Crociani.

With Ibrahim Samouiel at his home in Damascus. Photograph by Paola Crociani.

With Ezzeddin Ibrahim in Abu Dhabi. Photograph by Paola Crociani.

With Tayeb Saleh at the award ceremony of the Naguib Mahfouz Medal for Literature, AUC, Cairo. Photograph by Paola Crociani.

With Said al-Kafrawi at the author's home in Fayoum, Egypt. Photograph by Paola Crociani.

With Mohamed El-Bisatie at the author's home in Fayoum, Egypt. Photograph by Paola Crociani.

With Abdou Gubeir at the author's home in Fayoum, Egypt. Photograph by Paola Crociani.

With Yusuf Abu Rayya at the AUC Zamalek Bookstore, Cairo. Photograph by Paola Crociani.

With Mohamed Makhzangi at a restaurant in Cairo, Egypt. Photograph by Paola Crociani.

Mark Linz, Salwa Bakr, Said al-Kafrawi, and the author at the AUC Press fortieth anniversary dinner in 2000.

With Mohamed al-Murr in Abu Dhabi. Photograph by Paola Crociani.

With Hanan al-Shaykh at her home in London. Photograph by Paola Crociani.

With Amira Abu al-Magd at the Frankfurt Book Fair, 2004. Photograph by Paola Crociani.

With Edwar al-Kharrat at the Frankfurt Book Fair, 2004. Photograph by Paola Crociani.

11

Whenever I needed to find another job I would return to London before going out again to the Middle East. But the time came when the American oil company for whom I worked as their local representative in Qatar decided to pull out, and I was once more looking for employment, but this time my knowledge of Arabic failed to find me work. In great part I had only myself to blame, as I stubbornly refused to commit myself to anything that looked like giving me a career. I had already refused an offer in Qatar to join Shell and I had also, long since, turned down the possibility of making a career in the foreign service. I even, on returning from Qatar, applied for a job as the Middle East representative for Max Factor, but after the first interview it was clear to both sides that a marriage between us would not be a happy one. So, living in London and unable to find a job in the Middle East, I was prevailed upon by my father to continue with my studies of law. This I did by correspondence course—not the ideal way for endearing one to any form of learning.

My dislike of living in England rather than, for instance, Egypt was confirmed to me shortly after I arrived back in 1954, as I passed one morning by the kiosk where I bought my daily packet of cigarettes (thankfully no longer a requirement). Searching through my pockets, I found that I had changed suits and had no money. "I'll pay you tomorrow," I told the girl and stretched out my hand for the packet. But she was there before me and had retrieved the cigarettes. This told me that I was no longer in Egypt.

I stayed in London from 1954 until 1969. During the early part of that time I passed my law exams and practiced at the bar. While not unsuccessful, I was never happy in a wig and gown. I then formed a company called Middle East Services. It started off as a translation bureau, doing nothing but translations from Arabic. Mainly I was doing legal and commercial documents—and nothing is more soul-destroying. But soon the opportunity came to produce the quarterly literary magazine that I called *Aswat*, and my office thus became something of a home-from-home for Arab writers visiting London.

For a time I had corresponded with the Iraqi poet Badr Shakir al-Sayyab, one of the leaders of the modern movement in Arabic poetry. He was strongly anti-Communist and early on wrote me a letter criticizing me for featuring Picasso in the first issue of *Aswat*. He later contributed several poems, among them his famous poem about Jameela Bouhirid, the young girl who was tortured by the French in Algeria. Later, after I met him in London, he contributed several short poems in which, helpless before the cruel disease that was draining his body of health, he compared his fate to that of the biblical Job.

One morning I received a telephone call from him announcing that he had arrived in London, and he was staying at the Cumberland Hotel. As my office lay in a small street behind Selfridge's, the Cumberland Hotel was close by, and I invited him to call in at the office any time at his leisure, but he insisted that I should go to the hotel. I agreed to walk round to the hotel when I had finished work. At reception I asked for his room number and went up in the lift. I rang the bell of his room several times and was on the point of going downstairs again, thinking that perhaps I had been given the wrong room number. But I rang again and the door opened—it had simply taken Badr all that time to reach the door. He explained about the crippling illness from which he was suffering and about which he had consulted all the doctors of Beirut and elsewhere. Did I know of a good doctor? A day or so later I took him to see my doctor, James Bevan, but the verdict was what he had already heard from other doctors. Badr was booked into the Middlesex Hotel, where he had a series of painful tests on his vertebral column. James Bevan suggested to me that Badr was capable of accepting the hard truth, rather than being fobbed off with false hopes, so he was told that he had an incurably crippling disease affecting his backbone and that he should not waste time and money doing the rounds of yet more doctors. A few days later he took himself off to Kuwait, where he died at the age of 39. Recently I found several of his letters and one or two poems in his handwriting. I thought that my Iraqi friend Khalid al-Maali, who lives in Germany, might be interested to have them, and they have now been published in his magazine *'Uyun*.

Another writer I published in *Aswat* was Ghassan Kanafani. He and I first became friends not through meeting but through exchanging letters. I remember that he specifically asked me if we could correspond, as he needed someone with whom he could exchange ideas about writing. It was agreed that he would write to me in Arabic and that I would reply in English. His letters to me were handwritten, in a particularly neat and clear hand, while mine to him were perforce typewritten, because of my sometimes illegible handwriting. It was several years later that we met for the first time: it was at the Cleopatra Hotel in Cairo. I was with Ibrahim Shukrallah and we were chatting in Arabic. As we entered the hotel lobby, a handsome young man, perhaps hearing someone so obviously English talking Arabic, rose to his feet and came toward me: "You must be Denys," he said. "I'm Ghassan."

It was only later, in 1970, when I left Dubai and went to live in Beirut that I came to know Ghassan better. We would sometimes eat at a café just opposite the entrance to the American University of Beirut. I knew that he was deeply involved in the struggle for Palestine, but our conversation was invariably about literature and his hopes for Arabic writing. He contributed a short story to *Aswat*, and I included a story of his in the Oxford University Press collection of Arabic short stories. "The

Death of Bed No. 13" was derived from his early life when he was living in the Gulf; it was later republished in a collection of short stories in the United States, where the writer was described as coming from Jordan, although in my "Notes on Authors" it was definitely stated that he was Palestinian.

I translated another story by Ghassan—also inspired by his time in Kuwait—entitled "The Slave Fort" in my second volume of short stories from the Arab world, published by Quartet Books. When republished in the United States by Columbia University Press, the volume appeared with an introduction by a well-known Orientalist, who started off by stating that the names of the writers had been incorrectly given. He then provided two columns, one giving the name by which each writer appears in the volume, the other giving the names as—according to him—they should properly be written. It was as though I, the translator, didn't know the rules about transliterating Arabic characters into English. We thus find that Tayeb Salih—who has chosen to write his name in this way—is given as aṭ-Ṭayyib Ṣāliḥ in the second column. All this demonstrates is that such Orientalists appear to hold the belief that the only possible readers of translations from Arabic are students of the language. They are thus determined to keep modern Arabic literature in the academic cupboard for as long as possible. I, on the other hand, do not believe it really matters a damn whether Tayeb's name is as he has chosen to write it or whether it should, by the strict laws of transliteration, be written at-Tayyib. Readers have by now become used to a writer called Naguib Mahfouz, but the academics would like to introduce them instead to someone called Najib Mahfuz.

One evening Ghassan and I were driving around Beirut when a police patrol stopped us. "Don't talk in Arabic," he warned me—and the sad truth was brought home to me that as a foreigner in the Arab world one can be an object of suspicion if one happens to know the language. There are times when one should let it be known that one knows the language and others when one should not. In most instances at an airport, one should keep to one's own language. On one occasion I brought with me from Dubai a large water heater to install in my flat in Cairo. As I was passing through customs, I was asked what this object was. "It's a water heater," I responded, and then added in a very 'English' voice: "It's something that one fixes up in one's bathroom and which provides immediate hot water . . . ." The customs official, immediately realizing he was out of his depth with this voluble Englishman with the strange accent, quickly waved me through. "Welcome sir," he said with a bow, and he then turned to his colleague: "These tourists—God alone knows what they do with all this stuff they bring in!" An Arab friend of mine who had a French mother and traveled on a French passport enjoyed watching erotic films, and would always bring several with him when returning to his home in Cairo. One time, flashing his French passport and greeting the customs officials in French, he was waved through—but for his ill luck, an Egyptian friend happened to see him on his way out through customs and greeted him in Arabic. My friend was immediately called back and his baggage searched.

Nonetheless, there are certainly times when a knowledge of Arabic contained within the body of someone who could not look more English can be useful. Way back in 1949, on my way through Cairo to Tehran, I stayed for a few nights at the inexpensive Cosmopolitan Hotel. At that time all foreigners, even though passing through, had to register with the police. While the hotel had given me the appropriate form, I had forgotten all about it. I was then told by the man at the desk that a policeman had been around and that I should report to the nearest police station. I took a taxi to the police station. I was kept waiting for some time and was standing in front of the police officer, who had addressed me in English, explaining, in English, that I was very sorry about having forgotten to register, and so on and so forth. At that moment the taxi driver, whom I had asked to wait, put his head around the door and asked me whether he should continue to wait. I told him in Arabic that it seemed I would be there for some time and that he should go, and I paid him off. The officer immediately gave me a look of friendly surprise and ordered that a chair be brought for me. To this, on the spur of the moment, I replied: "*Tekerrisli ba'a?*" While this can simply mean "Are you providing me with a chair to sit on?" the expression is one used by smokers of hashish to mean: “Are you going to put me a piece of hashish on the pipe?”—it so happened that I had interested myself in the jargon used by hashish smokers and the poetry that had been written about the drug, which was widely used at that time. The effect of my words was electric: the officer slapped his forehead as a sign of disbelief, and immediately tore up the form he had been filling in ordering me to attend court. Having asked me how I wanted my coffee, he spent the next half hour talking with me about how expensive really good hashish was becoming.

On another occasion I was traveling by Middle East Airlines and landed up in Beirut without one of my suitcases. I went to the offices of the airline and complained to the girl at the desk. She could not have been less interested in my problem. While we were talking (in English), her boss came in and asked her, in Arabic, what the trouble was. “The fellow’s eating air,” she answered, meaning he’s wasting his time. “So I’m eating air, am I?” I asked the girl when her boss had left. My suitcase was found in double quick time!

Ghassan Kanafani was instrumental in insisting that I undertake the translation of some selections from the poetry of Mahmoud Darwish, the number one poet of the Palestinian resistance. In 1974, the three of us had lunch at the Barmaki restaurant in central Beirut. The task required me to read through all the poetry that Darwish had written up to that date, to make a selection, and to write an introduction. Even in those early years, Darwish’s poetry was often obscure, and I was helped out in understanding many of the more difficult lines by Elias Khouri, a Lebanese writer who had associated himself with the Palestinian struggle and Palestinian writing. I was later to translate and publish in the Libyan-funded literary magazine *Azure* (edited in London) part of an early novel by Elias Khouri. I published my selection of Darwish’s poetry under the title *Music of Human Flesh*, a phrase from one of the poems. It was my first and only venture into the realm of translating poetry, feeling that it takes a poet to translate poetry. I was later pleased to find that several of my translations were included in an American anthology called *The Vintage Book of Contemporary World Poetry*.

It was during this time in Beirut that somebody coming from Cairo brought me a copy of a novel entitled *That Smell*, the first novel by Sonallah Ibrahim. It was little more than a novella, but it impressed me right from the start. Containing as it did one or two frank scenes, the novel was banned by the Egyptian authorities. I translated it under the title *The Smell of It*, and it was published, together with several early short stories by the writer, in a slim volume in the Arab Authors series. Sonallah was to become one of Egypt's leading novelists.

Ghassan, like every Arab writer, was aware of how important it was to be translated. He was, I think, especially keen for me to translate his novel *Men in the Sun*. I didn't get around to it, but it was then perfectly adequately done by someone else. I felt that Ghassan hadn't at that stage achieved his full potential, and that in time he would produce some longer work that I would wish to translate. It was not to be. I had been with him a couple of evenings previous to my return to London. I was sitting in the airport lounge on my own and noticed that several Palestinians known to me were there. Before boarding, there was much agitated coming and going among the Palestinians. I discovered the reason for this only when I arrived in London and turned on the television, where the first item of news was the murder of Ghassan Kanafani, along with his young niece—they had been killed by a bomb placed under his car earlier that morning in 1972.

12

While living in London between 1954 and 1969 I got to know Tayeb Salih. Though we had both worked in the Arabic section of the BBC, we had never overlapped. I think that the first piece of his writing that I read was the short story "The Doum Tree of Wad Hamid." He submitted it to *Aswat* and I was immediately struck by the easy style and its underlying sense of humor. It was, to my mind, an excellent piece of writing. I immediately asked my friend and former colleague at the BBC, the Egyptian artist Abdel Salam Ali Nur, to do some illustrations for it, and he was inspired to do three black-and-white drawings that admirably reflected the atmosphere of the story, which told of a village on the banks of the Nile where the villagers—and visitors—were pestered by midges. I had always hoped to have an Arabic story translated by me published in *Encounter*. Having finished translating the story, I put it straight into an envelope and sent it to the magazine, and it came as no surprise when it was accepted for publication. Later, I published a further two of Tayeb's stories in the same magazine.

I then read and immediately translated his novella *The Wedding of Zein*, a tale of Sudanese village life, which I find a wholly successful piece of fiction. It was reviewed with enthusiasm by none other than the novelist Kingsley Amis. The novella was later made into a film by a Kuwaiti director, with Ibrahim al-Salahi—the artist who had drawn the cover for the Oxford volume of *Modern Arabic Short Stories*—taking on with rare professionalism the role of one of the main characters, the dervish holy-man who is central to village life.

Then came the day when Tayeb told me that he was starting on a new, more ambitious novel. It was written out in longhand, and every few days at my office I would receive a sheaf of papers, a further episode. Soon the novel, entitled *Season of Migration to the North*, was finished, with the translation completed at almost the same time. Tayeb was uncertain about some of the erotic passages contained in the novel, though there was nothing in them that would upset an English reader. He eventually decided to delete a few passages. For a time we thought of including them in the English translation, but rightly decided against it. Whereas it is not unknown for translators to omit the occasional passage—perhaps because they haven't quite understood it—it would be wholly unique for a translator to add some passages that weren't to be found in the original. Somewhere among my papers I possess these particular passages, written out in Tayeb's hand on two pages. One day they will perhaps find their way to an auction room and be bought up for a vast sum by some millionaire keen to acquire such a curiosity! Even without the debated passages, the novel found disfavor in several quarters, including the Sudanese government, which decided to ban it. I was confident that in this novel I had a work of Arabic fiction that should be able to find a home with some leading London publisher rather than in a series devoted to modern Arabic writing. But I had neither the necessary contacts nor the time and patience to send the manuscript to various publishers. It was just much easier to have it published in the Arab Authors series that I myself had created.

It is strange that, some fifteen or twenty years later, I translated another work of fiction by Tayeb entitled *Bandarshah*. I tried this new work out on Tom Maschler, the well-known editor at Jonathan Cape. He told me that he liked *Bandarshah* well enough, but if only I had sent in the manuscript of *Season of Migration* when I first translated it, he would, he suggested, have taken it at once and thenceforth would have published the rest of Tayeb Salih's work under the Jonathan Cape imprint. Nice words. It is significant that it required Naguib Mahfouz to be awarded the Nobel prize for literature before an Arab writer could get into a mainstream publisher's list—and even now the British reading public hasn't taken to him the way the Americans have.

Season of Migration to the North was published in its English translation in 1969, and several of London's critics were generous in their praise of it. In particular, Jill Neville, the book reviewer for *The Sunday Times*, chose the book as "the novel of the year." I happened to be in London at the time and I remember going into Hatchard's in Picadilly to ask for the book, expecting to find copies of it decorating one of the windows. But it needed, I'm sorry to say, more than Jill Neville and *The Sunday Times* for Tayeb Salih's novel to be regarded as other than a competent piece of writing coming out of Africa. When I inquired in Hatchard's about the book by its title, I was greeted with a blank stare. I then mentioned the author's name, which also didn't elicit a response. He's an Arab writer, I explained. "Oh yes, sir, well you'll find him down in the basement." It has taken something like four decades for Tayeb's novel to make its way up from the basement in Hatchard's to being added to the Penguin Modern Classics. In the intervening years the novel came out in various paperback editions, both in Britain and in the United States. A new hardback edition of the novel was published by a small publisher in the States called Michael Kesend, to which I wrote an introduction and which was the runner-up for a literary prize. While sales of the novel in English were in the mere hundreds annually, it was at least being kept in print, which is more than can be said for many novels published that long ago.

In the meantime the novel has been translated into twenty-one other languages. I obviously had nothing to do with any of these translations, though through them I was given an insight into the world of translation. When a Norwegian publisher decided to produce the novel, he asked permission of Heinemann to use the English translation, and I was paid some nominal fee; when the book appeared I was sent a copy in which it was stated that it had been translated from my English translation. In the case of the Japanese translation, I was approached by the translator, who possessed a good knowledge of Arabic, and asked whether I had any objection to his making use of my translation. This is the only time that a translator has frankly made such a request (which I was obviously only too happy to agree to). What translator, knowing that a certain book has already been translated into English, has such scruples that he or she doesn't refer to that translation? In fact, in several instances translators have definitely worked from my translation rather than from the original. When it came to the Spanish translation of Tayeb's novel, the Spanish publisher started out by indicating that he wished to have the novel translated from the English, and Heinemann wrote and told me so. Then the publisher changed his mind and said that the translation would after all be made straight from the Arabic. When the novel came out I asked for a copy and saw that several minor changes I had made in my translation—with the author's agreement—had mysteriously also found their way into the Spanish translation! Another, more blatant case relates to a volume of short stories I translated by the Egyptian writer Salwa Bakr. Among the stories it contained was one for which both she and I had mislaid the Arabic original—and yet the story was later to appear in various translations purported to have been made from the Arabic!

The time came when a literary agent indicated that he could perhaps sell the film rights to *Season of Migration to the North*. I have always felt that here was a novel that could make an intelligent and exciting film, a film that could appeal both to western and Arab audiences. I remember seeing *Tora! Tora! Tora!*, a film about the Japanese attack on Pearl Harbor, where the Japanese characters spoke Japanese and the Americans English, and the film was provided with subtitles. I thought it worked very well, and feel that *Season of Migration to the North* could be produced in the same way, with the central character played by an Arab actor with a good knowledge of English. I was in Cairo at the time when the subject was first mooted, and I still have the telegrams that were sent to me about the sums of money proposed. Later I was in a village in Sussex, where at one time I spent most weekends, and I received a phone call from somebody wishing to discuss the possibility of making the film. The phone call went on for sometime, and I was continually being interrupted by my wife calling me to lunch. At last I came off the phone. She inquired who it was, and I replied that it was someone called Franco Zeffirelli. The name, I confess, meant nothing to me! Anyway, nothing transpired, though I later heard that none other than Harold Pinter was to write the scenario. What happened? I never found out. In 2005 I heard that a play has been written based on *Season*, to be put on in London by the Royal Shakespeare Company in front of a selected audience; if it is well received, it will go into a public production.

If Tayeb has a fault it is that he hasn't written more. Quite a few years went by before he published two further books dealing with some of the same characters that had appeared in *The Wedding of Zein* and *Season of Migration to the North*, called *Maryoud* and *Bandarshah*. The author himself has told me he considers them to contain some of his best writing, and I would agree that the two books contain episodes that are as good as anything he has written. For the first time, though, I had difficulty translating his work. It seemed to me—and I told him so—that the two latest books didn't 'hold together.' Tayeb assured me that he was planning a further two volumes and that these would tie up the whole story that he wanted to recount. Tayeb was at that time adviser to Qatar's Ministry of Information, and I went out and stayed several weeks in Doha while I tried to sort out my translation of the two books with him. It was decided that they should be published in a single volume by Katharine Salahi, the English wife of Ibrahim al-Salahi, who had started up a publishing company. However, by the time the book was ready for publication, her company had gone into bankruptcy, and the book was eventually published by an unenthusiastic Routledge and Kegan Paul, to almost complete critical silence. Then, many years later in 2004, Tayeb Salih was awarded Egypt's State Prize for Literature for *Season of Migration to the North*.

Through Tayeb Salih I had got to know the Sudanese ambassador in London, Jamal Mohamed Ahmed. A graduate of Oxford, he was a man of great charm and rare accomplishment who later became his country's minister of foreign affairs. He was also a writer with several publications to his name. He had a special interest in the achievements of Africans in the domain of creativity and contributed a long article to *Aswat* on Negritude.

By then he had become a friend, and I felt able to seek his help in a personal matter. My father, unable to put off any further the date of his retirement as the secretary of a trade association concerned with retail price maintenance, suddenly applied, to the horror of his wife, for a post as lecturer in law at Khartoum University. He had had a happy few years in Sudan in the 1920s, and he now had a dread of being retired—on the other hand, his much younger wife could think of nothing more terrible than to leave her house and garden in Rickmansworth for the deserts of Sudan. However, being more than sixty-five, the authorities at Khartoum University replied that though well enough qualified, he was too old for the job. My father was desperate and asked me to see if my friend the ambassador couldn't 'pull strings.' I knew that I was asking Jamal the impossible, but I nevertheless sought his help. He did his best for, as he once said of me, "the only white Sudanese," but he was unsuccessful. My father went to live in the Canary Islands and died there, largely, I believe, of sheer boredom.

Many years later, when I had begun to write children's books, I persuaded the publisher Andy Smart, who had spent time as a teacher in an out-of-the-way part of Sudan, to publish a book of *Tales from Sudan*. The main story in it I took from Jamal Mohamed Ahmed's book *Sali Fu Hamr*, a volume of traditional tales taken from various African countries. I adapted the title story and made of it the cornerstone of my book of Sudanese stories for children; it was a traditional story taken from Sudan's long past history—only now excavations in the northern province are showing how advanced a civilization was flourishing in this remote corner of the world. By chance I found the same story—a story as enthralling as that of Sheherezade in *The Thousand and One Nights*—recounted again by the Italian author Roberto Calasso in his book *The Ruins of Kasch*.

13

Yusuf Idris was a charismatic character and a writer of great talent. In the Oxford University Press volume of *Modern Arabic Short Stories*, I had chosen a story that he later turned into a play but that, in retrospect, did not reveal his real genius as Egypt's master of the short story. Perhaps it was that he had as yet not written his best work. Yusuf, for all his charm, had, at times, an embarrassingly exaggerated view of his position as a writer. He once told me, in all seriousness, that I had made a big mistake in not dedicating my whole time and talents to translating his work. To this I made some ribald response; happily, Yusuf had a good sense of humor and was capable of laughing at himself. However, in a way he was right: Yusuf needed not necessarily me but someone who would have made a point of producing a standard translation of his work. As it was, his stories appeared, translated by different hands, in various anthologies, and volumes of his stories came out in English translation in both the United States and Britain, but there was no definitive edition of his work.

His few novels did not attract much attention, and it was only recently that an early novel of his was translated into English by Neil Hewison under the title *City of Love and Ashes*. When I was consulted about a possible Arab writer to be nominated for the Nobel prize, Yusuf's name was on the list of candidates. Let it be said that in the eyes of many younger Arab writers, Yusuf Idris was at one time held in higher regard than Naguib Mahfouz. It was therefore not unnatural for Yusuf Idris to entertain the hope that, when it came to it, he would be the Arab candidate for the Nobel prize. But various factors worked in Mahfouz's favor, not least his extraordinarily large output and the fact that his work, mainly as a novelist, was more readily available in English and French translation.

Yusuf Idris, like Tewfik al-Hakim, Naguib Mahfouz, and Louis Awad, was employed at Egypt's top newspaper, al-Ahram. His travels abroad included many trips to Russia. He told me that his novel *al-Haram* had been translated into Russian in a print run of more than a million copies. Why, he was continually asking, didn't his writings sell more in English translation? He was disappointed that in Arabic too his writings did not have the sort of sales he wanted, but then whose writings did? At one time he suggested to me that he should start writing in English, so that he could have the sort of readership he deserved. To this, I tried, as gently as possible, to point out that his English, learned at school and during his medical studies, had a long way to go before he could write creatively in it.

During periodic trips to London he would come to my office and we would often go out to lunch. He was extraordinarily jealous of anyone who might be seen to be competing with him. He was in London when the issue of *Aswat* containing Tayeb Salih's story "The Doum Tree of Wad Hamid" came out. He was outspokenly critical of me for accepting "such a poor story." To which I retorted that he of all people should be able to recognize a good short story when he read one. But Yusuf was not one to take umbrage, and we laughed the whole matter off. Yusuf had become a personal friend and would visit me in my flat in London. Once, knowing that there was an avant-garde play on at the Royal Court, I booked seats. The play, as it turned out, was as full of four-letter words as any I'd seen, and ended with an explicit sexual scene. I was embarrassed for my wife, who had accompanied us. Yusuf seemed unmoved by the whole performance and merely said to me later on that there was something he hadn't understood: what was this word 'sheet' they kept on using? I explained what 'shit' meant, grateful that his questioning didn't go beyond this!

My years in London were made bearable by the various trips abroad that came my way, often acting as interpreter for businessmen going to Saudi Arabia or the Gulf, or through holidays taken mainly in Morocco. On one occasion I was to be interpreter on a trip to Qatar, a place in which I had spent a year of my life when it was still one of the least visited places on earth. I was therefore only too happy to go back and see what changes had taken place. The task at hand was to help negotiate a contract with the ruler for the making of a documentary film about the sheikhdom, which was just emerging from obscurity. The person I was to accompany was the head of one of the leading documentary film companies in London. I was already aware that my job in Qatar would most likely be rendered more difficult by the fact that this man was known to be an alcoholic, and that we were going to this ultra-strict country in Ramadan. An indication of the extent of my charge's trouble was given when, after we were shown to our seats in first class, he immediately ordered a double whisky for himself and asked me what I'd be having. I said that, to start with, I would like to have some breakfast. During the flight he informed me that he was carrying a couple of bottles of whisky and would there be any trouble about getting them into the country? I told him that no country in the world was drier than Qatar, and I also reminded him that we were in the holy month of Ramadan, when drinking would be even more frowned upon.

At Doha airport I made a great show of my Arabic and indicated that once, way back in 1950, I had spent a year in the place, and how glad I was to be back, and what an important person I was accompanying, and that early next morning we would have the honor of meeting the ruler. With a heavy sigh of relief I saw our bags being scribbled over with white chalk. Nothing remained for me to do except to see that my companion was in a more or less fit state when we had meetings with the ruler. He left for London with an agreement on the film, though wondering what possible aspects of this dull and as yet underdeveloped community could be incorporated into a documentary, while I stayed on for a couple of nights. On my way back in the plane, sitting in an aisle seat and trying to finish some commercial translation job I had brought out with me, I found a man standing at my elbow, greeting me. It was Ezzeddin Ibrahim, an Egyptian I had met in Doha who was working for the Qatari Ministry of Education. He mentioned that he had recently read my translation of Tewfik al-Hakim's play *The Tree Climber* and liked it. We both expressed the hope that we might meet someday somewhere.

Several years later, during the period when I was traveling around the countries of the Gulf as a representative for firms of architects and consulting engineers, I found that Ezzeddin had in the intervening years given up his job in Qatar, taken a doctorate from London University (with Bob Serjeant), been for a while professor of Arabic Literature at Riyadh University, and was now cultural advisor in Abu Dhabi to Sheikh Zayed, the late president of the United Arab Emirates. On a business trip to Abu Dhabi I went to see him in his offices in the picturesque Old Fort, one of the few buildings that have been allowed to remain from Abu Dhabi's past. There I found that Ezzeddin's assistant was Ali Riyad, who had been one of my students at Cairo University. During my few days' stay in Abu Dhabi, Ezzeddin gave me a copy of *Riyad al-salihin*, a well-known collection of Hadith (the Prophet's Sayings) by an-Nawawi. When I returned the book and said that I had found much of the material fascinating—at university only the Qur'an had been required reading—Ezzeddin then proposed to me that we should work together on producing an English translation of a smaller collection of Hadith by the same author, known as *An-Nawawi's Forty Hadith*. He expressed the view that the ideal method for translating religious texts—texts that required above all else complete accuracy—was for two people to cooperate, a translator whose native tongue was English and who yet had a good knowledge of Arabic, together with another scholar whose native language was Arabic but who also possessed a good knowledge of

English. I was to deal with the initial draft translation, which we would then go through together. Owing to the fact that we both led busy lives and were seldom to be found together at one place, we would snatch meetings as and where we could.

The book was eventually completed. Ezzeddin was visiting Beirut at the time—it was in the early 1970s, when I was living in the Lebanese capital—and we decided to publish the book with a Syrian friend of his, Bassam Ustwani, who was the owner of the Holy Koran Publishing House. The three of us each contributed £1,500 to the venture, and I remember thinking to myself that I might never see my investment again! However, the book was a great success and has gone into twenty editions, being later published by the Islamic Texts Society, which operates out of Cambridge, and again by Dar el Shorouk, Egypt's leading publishing house. It has achieved this success mainly through the efforts of Ezzeddin and the support of the then ruler of Abu Dhabi and others who sponsored various editions. In addition it has attracted the attention of a number of other publishers who have produced pirated editions.

Ezzeddin and I were thinking about what other book of Hadith to translate when chance provided us with the opportunity to meet up in one place for a period of time each year. This came about on one of my trips to Abu Dhabi. Ezzeddin and I were sitting at a café on Abu Dhabi's shoreline when he suddenly seized me by the arm and led me along to where Sheikh Zayed had just entered with a number of his retainers. Ezzeddin introduced me to the ruler as the person he was working with on translating Hadith and the ruler immediately suggested that I should be given accommodation in Abu Dhabi for two weeks each year, plus a yearly return ticket. This arrangement continued for several years and made it possible for us to produce our next book, a short selection made by ourselves of those special Hadith known as Hadith Qudsi, which are Sayings of the Prophet in which God expresses Himself through the mouth of His Prophet. We then turned our attention to a longer book of Hadith selected by the famous scholar Ibn Taymiyyah, entitled *The Goodly Word*.

I decided to try my hand alone at translating one of the books making up al-Ghazali's classical work *Ihya' 'ulum al-din* ('The Revivication of the Sciences of Religion'). I chose a short one on the subject of food and the teachings of Islam in regard to one's obligations as a host, table manners, and so on. For me it was a venture into the world of scholarly translation rather than that of the literary. I experienced difficulty with the text, but even more so with such matters as the notes, appendices, and bibliography that were demanded of me, and not least with the tracing of the many Prophetic Traditions contained in the work. Eventually I was helped by my friend Abdurrahman Fitzgerald, whom I had got to know in Marrakesh, and the book was published in 2000 by the Islamic Texts Society.

For our next project, Ezzeddin and I decided to take on a new translation of selected passages from the Qur'an brought together under separate headings according to subject matter. The Qur'an consists of 114 Suras (or chapters) of varying length dealing with a variety of subjects. We plan to name our translation *Readings in the Holy Qur'an*. While carrying out this translation we have obviously been curious to see, when in doubt about a passage, what other translators have made of it, and we have been struck by the extraordinary diversity in the translations. In a recent book of essays, the American Orientalist Bernard Lewis gives several examples of translations of a single verse of the Qur'an that differ so greatly that each translator appears to be dealing with a totally different verse. Is it not time, having accepted that the Qur'an is continually being given new translations, for al-Azhar University, for example, to gather together a body of scholars and produce, once and for all, a standard, 'official' rendering? Perhaps, though, al-Azhar has rightly refused to venture into such dangerous waters where, whatever the result, it can gain only adverse criticism.

Several years ago the ruler of Sharjah, Dr. Sheikh Sultan, decided to produce a recording on tape of the Qur'an, consisting of a recital in Arabic, followed by a reading in English translation of the verses just recited. I was asked by the ruler which translation should be used. I answered that of all the translations available, that of Marmaduke Pickthall, first published in 1930, remained perhaps the most suitable. An obvious plus for the Pickthall translation was that it had been done by an Englishman who had converted to Islam. Before, however, proceeding with the recording, several hundred changes were incorporated into the translation, where it was felt that it was not sufficiently accurate.

A team of us—an Egyptian Qur'an reciter, Sheikh Habba (an Azharite expert on the intricate rules regarding the recital of the Qur'an), a young English convert, Duncan Carse (a well-known professional reader of commentaries), Dr Ezzeddin, and I—all made our way to Athens, where the EMI studios would be doing the recording. Duncan Carse had been my choice for reading the translation of the Qur'an, but someone had whispered in the ruler's ear that the reader should be a Muslim. Ezzeddin had rightly pointed out that an English translation of the Qur'an was not, like the Arabic, the word of God, and that the criterion to be used in choosing a reader was professional competence. The ruler, however, did not wish to attract any criticism relating to the religion of the reader, so a young English convert had been found who would read the English translation under the guidance of Duncan Carse.

We all stayed at a hotel in central Athens and went off daily to the EMI studios, with Ezzeddin and Sheikh Habba supervising the recording of the Arabic, and Duncan Carse and I in charge of the English. Having spent a week at work, the recital of the Arabic was halfway into the Qur'an, while on the English we were still laboring with the first few pages. It soon appeared clear to Duncan and me that no amount of coaching would produce from the young reader the sort of result required. Ezzeddin therefore asked me if I didn't know an English Muslim who had recording experience. The name of Gai Eaton immediately came to mind. But where was Gai Eaton, and how to get in touch with him? While I had known Gai briefly at Cambridge, I was not in regular touch with him. By good fortune, his son was known to my wife, as he had done work for the Central Office of Information, Britain's equivalent of a ministry of information, where my wife was head of the films division. Some phone calls elicited the information that Gai's son and his wife were renting a villa somewhere on the island of Crete. My wife and I flew into Heraklion, from where we hired a car and drove around the villages until we located Gai's son, and through him were able to contact Gai himself, who later made the recording in London.

14

Toward the end of my time in London, the Central Office of Information decided to start a weekly quarter-hour television magazine program to be sent out to the various television stations in the Arab world, and I was asked to be in charge of it. I called it *Adwa' wa aswat* ('Lights and Voices'). The weekly program consisted of four or five short items that might be of interest to the Arab viewer. Interesting visitors to London sometimes featured in the program; thus a whole edition was devoted to Omar Sharif, and another to the singer Abd al-Halim Hafez. I vividly recollect the final program: everything seemed to go wrong, and the script wasn't ready for me to check through on time. "Don't worry," I was told, "we'll go through it in the studio before we begin rehearsals." But on turning up at the studio, I found that it had been arranged that the whole edition was to be devoted to an interview with me!

During the two years the program ran, we made two trips to the Middle East with a camera crew. The first was to the north of Morocco. The great medieval traveler Ibn Battuta had always fascinated me, and it was known that he had been born in Tangier and had also died there. (Later, in Cairo, I wrote a children's book about this attractively enigmatic character, who was born at the beginning of the fourteenth century and, though less famous than his European rival Marco Polo, far outstripped him in the vast distances he traveled). However, on arriving in Tangier, and inquiring at the tourist information office for the whereabouts of Ibn Battuta's tomb, I was met with blank stares. Perhaps the position is different today, but in the late 1960s Ibn Battuta's tomb was not a tourist site. Eventually, we were taken to an unimpressive tomb, and we filmed our story about him. One of the presenters of the program was a Lebanese called Omar Yamak, who happened to bear a striking resemblance to Marlon Brando. We were shooting an item somewhere near Tetouan when, to the amusement of the crew, somebody watching us came up to me and asked if I could get him the autograph of the famous American film star!

In 1969 I found myself no longer capable of living in England. How to escape from it—and where to—was the problem. By chance it was solved by one of Jabra's periodical visits to London. He gave a lecture at London University about modern Arabic literature, to which I was invited. He referred to me in the course of the lecture, after which, to my alarm, he asked me to say a few words. As I faced the audience, I saw that it included Jack Briggs, who had become a friend of mine during the year I had spent in Qatar in the early 1950s. As a result of our meeting up after all those years, I heard of a job going as the director of an Arabic broadcasting station in Trucial Oman—now the United Arab Emirates. The station was owned by the British government and I was made a first secretary on the understanding that my sole duties would be as director of the broadcasting station. The British government then decided to move out of Trucial Oman, and I advised that the station be handed over to Sheikh Rashid, the ruler of Dubai, the sheikhdom from which most of the advertising revenue was derived. Sheikh Rashid then asked me what I was being paid, and offered me double the salary if I would stay on and continue to run the radio station; having heard that I had also had experience with television, he told me that he would also wish me to set up and run a television station. As a further encouragement, he told me that I would be permitted to run my own advertising agency in the Emirates. I asked him why he should choose an Englishman to run an independent station that broadcast in Arabic. He laughed, in the way he had, and said that he didn't care if I was Chinese—he had seen that I could run and make a business out of a radio station, and that was enough for him. Perhaps I should have accepted his offer and become a rich man, but I felt it was time to move on, so I telephoned Yusuf al-Khal in Beirut and asked him to find me a flat there.

Yusuf al-Khal had started the influential publication *Shi'r* ('Poetry'), which published the work of modern poets from around the Arab world. Yusuf himself, who had spent many years in the United States and possessed an excellent command of English, was also a poet in his own right. The flat he found me happened to be in the same block as he himself lived in, so we saw a lot of each other and through him I got to know many Lebanese and other writers who were friends of his. These included Laila Baalabaki, a story by whom I translated and published in the Oxford University Press volume. The story, "Spaceship of Tenderness to the Moon," fairly innocuous by western standards, was later published in *The Penguin Book of Erotic Short Stories by Women*. Before this, Laila had faced all sorts of trouble in Beirut because of what was regarded as her outspoken writing, including being taken to court for using a two-letter word (equivalent to one of our four-letter words) that happens to be one of the words most widely mouthed by the population of Lebanon.

Yusuf al-Khal was a great bon viveur, and his flat, with the small garden to the front, was always full of Lebanese friends and anyone from abroad who might be visiting Beirut, so long as they had an interest in Arabic writing. I first met the Moroccan writer Mohamed Zefzaf there, while Zakaria Tamer from Damascus—who has turned out to be one of the best short story writers in Arabic—was launched on his writing career by Yusuf, who published his first volume, *The Neighing of the White Steed*, from which I took a story for the Oxford volume. Zakaria Tamer later moved to London and I produced a representative volume of his work under the title *Tigers on the Tenth Day* with Quartet Books. My latest volume of Arabic short stories, published by the American University in Cairo Press under the title *Under the Naked Sky*, also contains a story by him.

Yusuf al-Khal felt it was time that someone made an anthology of modern Arabic poetry in English translation, and suggested that he and I should do it together. Poetry, however, hasn't been my prime interest, in addition to which Yusuf held the belief that most Arabic poetry needed heavy editing, and that all too many poems would be improved by drastic pruning. I, on the other hand, hold the view that it is not up to a translator to 'improve' any piece of writing, by either adding to it or deleting from it, though—Heavens knows!—one is often tempted to do so. While preparing my volume of Naguib Mahfouz's short stories for the AUC Press and Doubleday, I felt that the very short and delightful story "Half a Day" could do with an extra two words at the end. I rang Naguib with the suggestion and was not surprised when he agreed wholeheartedly to the addition in my English translation. Despite the award to him of the world's most prestigious literary prize, Naguib Mahfouz remains wholly free of any pretensions.

Yusuf was always hard up yet always seemed to have the money to enjoy the best of food and drink. He also bought, while I was there, a weekend place in the village of Ghazeer. He then found a cheap place for me to buy in the same village, intrigued as he was by the thought that someone who was making a new translation of several of the Gospels into Arabic should be the neighbor of an Englishman engaged on translating some of the Prophet's Hadith into English, an endeavor that I had just begun with my Egyptian friend from Abu Dhabi, Ezzeddin Ibrahim. Attractive and reasonably priced though the house and garden in Ghazeer was, I felt that Lebanon in the long run was not my place and that I would eventually return to live in Egypt.

Some years later, in London, I heard that Yusuf was seriously ill. He had sought treatment in Paris for the dread illness that comes to so many smokers. It was to no avail, and when Yusuf later came to London I met a man who was a shadow of my friend and neighbor in Beirut. It was not long before he died.

Hanan al-Shaykh became known to me when she published her first novel, *The Story of Zahra* with Quartet Books. It was obvious that here was a writer who, living in London, was able to stand back from the Arab scene and write about it as it impinged on the west. Perhaps what modern Arabic writing lacks, at least for it to become more widely read in the west, is a sense of it belonging to a larger whole. Most Arabs writing today have not lived abroad and generally do not know a foreign language, so that their writing tends to be enclosed. Few Arabic novels, for instance, feature characters from other parts of the world. Hanan, though writing in Arabic—unlike, say, Ahdaf Soueif—nevertheless has windows open onto other worlds and has made a real readership for herself in the west, both in English translation and in translation to other languages. Her books are professionally marketed by one of London's leading publishers and she has also made a name for herself in the United States. She is less highly considered in the Arab world, where many feel that she does not truly represent the Arab point of view. I remember that at one time she was criticized for portraying such characters as a Moroccan prostitute practicing her trade in London, and another Arab character who was gay; she was accused of washing Arab dirty linen in public, as though no one was aware that Arab women sometimes become prostitutes or that some Arab men were gay.

When she first became established, Hanan asked me whether I would become her translator. I didn't want to be tied down, so I suggested Catherine Cobham, who has served her well over the years. I have, however, translated several of her short stories, as well as, I now recollect, a charming children's story about the habit among some Arab women of using henna to decorate their hands and feet. For some reason Hanan has discontinued writing for children, though she clearly has a talent for it and would readily find a publisher in London for such stories.

In London, Hanan is acquainted with many of England's leading writers. One day she asked me to lunch because the critic and novelist Jill Neville wanted to meet me. I too wanted to meet her, for it was she, when she had been book critic of *The Sunday Times*, who had chosen Tayeb Salih's *Season of Migration to the North* as book of the year. Hardly had we sat down when Jill Neville turned to me and asked: "Hanan tells me you were teaching at Cairo University in the late forties. Did you by any chance know somebody called Peter Duval Smith?" "Yes, of course," I answered innocently. "He and I were the greatest of friends. We once shared a villa together in a suburb of Cairo called Maadi." I was somewhat taken aback when she responded: "You'd have to travel a long way to find a bigger bastard!" I showed my surprise, to which she replied: "You see, I knew Peter rather well—in fact I was married to him for several months." She then recounted how she had written a novel entitled *Fall Girl*, which was largely about her relationship with Peter. Before publishing it she felt that she should consult him, so she gave him the manuscript to read. He took it away and then returned it by throwing it at her with the words: "You can do what the hell you like with it, including having a picture of my cock on the cover!"

15

In 1974 I left Beirut to return to Cairo. Lebanon was just getting itself into a civil war, and I had already had some experience of how difficult life would become there. I bought a flat in Dokki, a fairly central district, under a system whereby, for a small lump sum, you got basic furniture and the freehold for yourself and direct family, but continued to pay a nominal rent.

It was about this time that I made the acquaintance of Yahya Taher Abdullah, one of the literary world's stranger characters. He had come up from his native town of Karnak in Upper Egypt to try to make his way in Cairo. I think I had first read a story by him in *Gallery 67*, the magazine edited by Edwar al-Kharrat, who was one of the first to recognize the young man's talents, and used his close relationship with the writer and one-time minister of culture Yusuf Sibai to gain a small monthly stipend for Yahya. Even so, Yahya lived a hand-to-mouth existence, and when I first met him he was sharing a tiny room with a boy who made a precarious living shining people's shoes. Reading his stories, I wondered what an English reader would make of them, yet I felt that some of his work should be made available in translation. As adviser to the Arab Authors series, I had almost carte blanche there. I showed one or two stories to James Currey, who, with Keith Sambrook, looked after both the African Writers and the Arab Authors series, and he needed no convincing that here was a writer who should be represented.

During the time I was working on the book, Yahya would often drop in at my flat in Dokki, sometimes with his young daughter. The first thing would be a raid on my fridge, and then I'd sit him down to answer any queries I had. "In one story," he told me "you'll find there's an inconsistency." "I know," I answered him. "What can we do about it?" "Nothing at all," he answered, "I like it that way." Luckily, readers generally don't notice inconsistencies. Then he asked me how much he would be paid. I said that it depended on how well the volume sold, that the publisher's contract would stipulate that the author and the translator would split the royalties fifty/fifty. Never one to mince his words, he immediately replied: "But you're only the translator!" In reply I dumped his stories into his lap with the words: "Then find yourself another translator," and explained that this was the arrangement for payment. He was immediately full of apologies. "Uncle Denys," he quickly assured me, using a common term of endearment and respect for an older man, "I'm just happy to know that my stories will be read in English—and that they are translated by you."

I was keen, in the case of Yahya's book, that it should come out in a hardback edition first of all. The books in the Arab Authors series were being published in paperback and were receiving very little critical attention, possibly in part due to the fact that being in paperback gave the impression that they had already appeared in hardback. James Currey promised me that the book would come out in hardback provided I could obtain orders from organizations in Cairo for a minimum of three hundred copies. Among the people who signed a request for a hundred copies was the poet Salah Abdul Sabour, whom I happened to know and who was the head of one of Egypt's governmental literary organizations. But by the time I required the pledge to be honored, Salah had died, at a comparatively young age. I thus went to see the establishment man who had taken over, who right away told me, "But Salah Abdul Sabour is dead," and returned the paper with his signature. "And you and I," I told him, "shall both die after, God willing, a long life." And I got up, leaving my coffee undrunk. I have since learned that Salah had little respect for Yahya either as a person or a writer, and it says a lot for him that he had, in his official capacity, given him his support.

Many years later, I translated a simplified version Salah had made for children of the well-known *Hayy Ibn Yaqzan* by Ibn Tufayl, a religious piece of writing that was translated very early on into English and was said to have inspired Defoe to write Robinson Crusoe. Salah Abdul Sabour's version had been published in Arabic many years back with delightful illustrations by the well-known Egyptian artist Mostafa Hussein. It had been published by Shorouk, the present publishers of my children's books, and so it was possible for me to do a rendering into English of the Arabic and for the book to be published under the title *Alone on a Desert Island.*

Still on the trail of a hardback edition for Yahya's stories, I also went to see Tewfik al-Hakim in his office at *al-Ahram*. Didn't he know someone of influence in the government who might give me an order for copies? He shook his head. However, Salah Taher, the artist who had designed the cover for the volume of the playwright's *Fate of a Cockroach*, happened to be in the room at the time. He rebuked Tewfik al-Hakim: Why didn't he ring up So-and-so, a deputy minister of culture. Obediently, Tewfik al-Hakim did so and obtained an appointment for me. But the interview was a disaster: the deputy minister started off by asking me why I was wasting my time translating the work of such a vagabond? I answered that I wasn't concerned whether Yahya was a vagabond or not, only that, in my opinion, he was a writer of real talent. The deputy minister obviously didn't agree. This time I finished my coffee and took my leave.

Though I didn't obtain the required number of orders, Heinemann nevertheless produced a hardback of the volume, under the title *The Mountain of Green Tea and Other Stories*. Unhappily, though, just as I was correcting the proofs of the introduction I had written, I received a telegram from my friend the writer Gamil Ibrahim Atia, telling me that Yahya Taher Abdullah had been killed in a car crash: a tire had burst, and he had thrown himself from the passenger seat, only then to be crushed by the car. None of the other occupants of the car, including his young daughter, was harmed. With the encouragement of a volume of his stories in English translation, Yahya's writing might well have taken on a new lease of life. He was 39 years of age and was full of talent. *The Mountain of Green Tea* is still in print with the AUC Press.

The gulf that exists in Egypt between those who produce literature and those who are supposed to encourage it widens with the years. Things came to a head in 2003 when it was decided to give the State Prize for Literature to the novelist Sonallah Ibrahim. Having appeared to accept the prize, he rejected it at the ceremony itself, saying that he wanted nothing to do with a government that lacked credibility. As enthusiastic as the audience had been when it was announced that Sonallah was the winner of the prize, their enthusiasm was even warmer when he rejected it. The next time it came for the prize to be awarded, anxious to spare themselves a similar embarrassment, the powers-that-be asked those in the running for the prize to sign a statement that, if offered the prize, they would accept it without causing any trouble. Several writers, notably Gamal al-Ghitani, Baha Taher, and the Lebanese Elias Khouri refused to sign such a statement. In the event, the next prize went to Tayeb Salih.

Some years back I read a collection of Egyptian stories by women writers. One story stood out: "My World of the Unknown" by Alifa Rifaat, a name I had not heard of. An unusual story with sexual undertones, it later found its way into *The Penguin Book of Erotic Short Stories by Women*. I remember meeting Alifa at Shepheard's Hotel, where we drank coffee and I told her how impressed I was by her story. The wife of a senior police officer and a deeply religious woman, she was an unlikely candidate for encouragement by those who had influence in the literary world, who for the most part had leftist leanings. She had already faced, it seems, a certain amount of antagonism from those around her because of her writing ambitions. She confided to me that she would like nothing better than to be translated into English. I asked to see other examples of her writing, and eventually I published some of her stories in a literary magazine, which resulted in her being invited to London (her first journey out of Egypt). Later, I translated a collection of her stories that was published by Quartet Books under the title *Distant View of a Minaret*; it achieved a certain success in England and America, though the English-language volume is now banned in Egypt because of the frankness with which some of the stories are written. She died in 1995.

I have never worried about whether a writer was well known, being always on the lookout for new talent. I find translation exacting work, and it is not well paid, so there seems to be little point in translating books of which one does not have a high opinion. Thus a number of friends in the Arab world often point me in the direction of younger and as yet unknown writers. It was in this way that I discovered the stories of the Iraqi writer Mohamed Khudayyir, who is represented in my last two collections of stories from the Arab world. A story by another Iraqi writer was given to me by Abdou Gubeir, a friend from early days, who is a writer and critic—one of his stories is to be found in *Under the Naked Sky*—and today he is my neighbor in the village overlooking Lake Qarun in which I have a much-loved straggling village house and some hundred or so olive trees. I remember with affection that he was one of those who strove to alert the establishment to the role that the Arab Authors series was playing in bringing modern Arabic literature to the attention of readers of English—but in this, like others, he was unsuccessful. I also remember that shortly after meeting him—through our mutual friend Desmond Stewart, one of the earliest supporters of the modern renaissance in Arabic literature—Abdou had told me frankly that he was in need of money, and would I be so good as to spare the time to do an interview with him? This was a refreshing change from the usual approach of journalists, who seek to persuade one that they are doing one a great favor. Later on, before he went to work in Kuwait, Abdou was the editor of the literary magazine *al-Qahira*, and he drew my attention to a story he had recently published by a certain Inaam Kachachi. He knew nothing about her except that she was an Iraqi journalist who lived in Paris. Having read the story and liked it, I translated it for inclusion in *Under the Naked Sky*. It then happened that she passed through Cairo and I had the opportunity of meeting her. What else had she written? I was surprised to hear that it was her only short story, but that she was working on a novel. The following summer I spent a few days in Paris and through Inaam met the Tunisian writer Habib Selmi. I had translated a story by Selmi for a general volume of short stories from the Arab world that I compiled in 1983. I had also translated a short novel by him entitled *Goat Mountain*, which I did not get published at the time. I later saw a French translation of the novel, which encouraged me to look through my papers, but I have been unable to find my translation. As a translator one translates much more than one publishes: sometimes one works on something and halfway through one suddenly has doubts and abandons it, or for one reason or another one cannot find a publisher for some piece of writing about which one was sufficiently enthusiastic at the time.

In Cairo a number of literary conventions are held and people are invited from near and far. Listening to lectures has always seemed to me a subtle form of torture that I can do without: I cringe at the sight of the man or woman making their way to the stage clasping a vast bundle of sheets from which they will tediously read, taking particular care to get all the case endings right and not to make any grammatical howlers. Just as I am loath to attend lectures by other people, I am equally against giving lectures myself, particularly in Arabic. I remember vividly the experience, when I was in Cairo in the 1940s, of attending a stultifyingly boring lecture by a distinguished Orientalist, and noticing that the Egyptian sitting alongside me appeared to be taking notes—but not at all: he was marking down the number of errors being committed by the great Orientalist in the course of his lecture!

At a soiree held by Maysoon Saqr, a young poet from the Emirates whom I had met at the office of Hosni Suleiman, founder of the Sharqiyat publishing house in Cairo, I found myself sitting next to a poet and novelist from Jordan called Ibrahim Nasrallah, who was employed by an organization in Amman called the Abdul Hameed Shuman Institute. He invited me to go to Amman, and I at once told him that I would not give a lecture but I was quite prepared to answer impromptu questions from an audience. The question and answer session went all right; interestingly for me, it was attended by a Palestinian who had worked with me some thirty years previously, when I had been in charge of an Arabic broadcasting station in what is now the United Arab Emirates.

On the first evening in Amman a dinner was arranged, at which the distinguished Palestinian critic and scholar Ihsan Abbas was a guest. It gave me great pleasure to see him again, for it was no less than fifty years since we had last met. Though we are of similar age, I had in fact been his teacher at Cairo University. I had been given the task of teaching English in the Arabic department, on the assumption that my knowledge of Arabic could be of help to the students. It quickly became apparent to me that Ihsan's knowledge of English was excellent and would not benefit from his spending a whole year reading through the one set book, *Great Expectations*. I therefore took him aside at the end of the class and told him not to trouble to attend any further classes but to read, if he had the time, a list of books that included among others *The Dubliners* and a novel by Virginia Woolf. It was many years later that someone showed me a copy of Ihsan's autobiography, where he mentions my fiction list and how this had attracted him to read further in English literature. In Amman we reminisced about the early days in Cairo. He told me about his only venture into translation, when he had accomplished the not inconsiderable task of translating *Moby Dick* into Arabic, and how ever since then he has had people telling him what an excellent translation it was, but wouldn't it have been better if, on page so-and-so, he had rendered this particular word or phrase by such-and-such?! It is one of the ways—of which there are all too many—in which the translator's task is a pretty thankless one. How often does somebody come up and say "I just loved your translation of So-and-so"? This has happened to me just the once, when James Currey of Heinemann, who knew no Arabic, congratulated me on using the phrase 'hanky panky' in my translation of

Tayeb Salih's *Season of Migration to the North*. On the other hand, once during a class at the American University in Cairo, a young woman, with many apologies and blushings, pointed out that even the best translator can make 'slips.' She then told me that somewhere or other I had made the most extraordinary mistake in translating *al-juma'a al-hazina* (literally, 'Sad Friday') as Good Friday. How had I made such an obvious error? I pointed out that I hadn't made a mistake, but that in English the day was indeed known as Good Friday. However, she continued to shake her head in disbelief as she sat down.

Recently Peter Clark, an Arabist and a translator interested in modern Arabic literature, who had been director of the British Council in Damascus, arranged for my wife and myself to visit Damascus and Aleppo. In each city I was required to meet local writers and to address them about the efforts being made to introduce modern Arabic writing to the English-speaking world. Thus it was, in Aleppo, that I had the opportunity to meet for the first time two writers whose stories I had included in the very first volume of Arabic short stories published with Oxford University Press. Abdel Salam Al-Ujaili was a prolific writer, a full-time practicing doctor, and had at different times been a minister. The story I had translated by him was entitled *The Dream* and revolved around a verse of the Qur'an. When translating it, I had immediately doubted his attribution of the verse to the chapter of al-Fath. On looking it up, I found that I was right, and that it was from the much shorter and better known chapter of al-Nasr. Unwilling to make the correction without consulting him, I wrote to him and pointed out the error as tactfully as possible—after all, he had been Minister of Culture. He wrote me back a letter of thanks, and years later I read an article by him in an issue of the magazine *Doha* referring to the gaffe he had made and pointing out that it had taken an Orientalist (not a description of myself that I care for) to discover the error. The story, he pointed out, had not only been published in a volume but had appeared in a number of magazines and had also been broadcast over Syrian radio and the BBC Arabic service—all without anyone noticing the mistake. Abdel Salam Al-Ujaili came from the nearby town of Raqqa, where he has his medical practice, and we spent an entertaining evening together. Waleed Ikhlassi, the other Syrian writer included in the Oxford volume, I saw only fleetingly because he was just off to Jordan to undergo an operation.

On my return to Damascus from Aleppo I made the acquaintance of one of Syria's younger writers of short stories, Ibrahim Samouiel, and we spent several enjoyable evenings at his flat at which young Japanese men and women were continually calling—Ibrahim had cornered the market in giving Arabic lessons to the Japanese living in Damascus. I included a story by him in my latest collection, *Under the Naked Sky*, in which, I notice, Syrian writers are not well represented, though of course Zakaria Tamer, now a resident of England, once again has a place.

16

Some of my life has been spent in the Gulf, and more particularly in what are now the United Arab Emirates, and I have long wanted to produce a volume of short stories from the area. I have read many of the stories of the Dubai writer Mohamed al-Murr, but found that two volumes had already been produced of his work in English translation, one by Peter Clark and the other by my friend of long ago in Qatar, Jack Briggs. I am still waiting for Mohamed to produce a novel about Dubai and the way it has progressed in a matter of fifty years from being a trading entrepôt, from which dhows laden with gold were smuggled into India, to the high-rise metropolis it has become today. I was once given the rare opportunity, way back in 1950 when I was living in Qatar, to pay a short visit to Dubai. I went there to interpret on behalf of the ruler, Sheikh Said, the father of Sheikh Rashid and grandfather of the present Sheikh Mohamed, in negotiations he was having with an oil company. It was explained to me that I would not be paid a fee as the sheikhdom was still poor, but it was sufficient reward for me to spend a few days in a Dubai that had remained unchanged for so long and has then only recently decided to challenge the rest of the world with its towering buildings and to enter the tourist stakes. There was of course no hotel in Dubai then, and I had stayed with Ron Codrai, the chronicler on camera of those days, together with Wilfred Thesiger, of this part of the world.

Nowadays I visit Abu Dhabi twice a year and always spend a few days in Dubai as Mohamed al-Murr's guest. During one of my recent visits he told me that he had decided to read through the whole literary output of Naguib Mahfouz, and that he was greatly impressed. I have promised myself that I will find the time to look around among the writers in the Emirates for sufficient material for a volume of short stories. I am being helped in this by my friend Kamel Yusuf Hussein, who has for long been a journalist in Dubai, and who has followed the literary scene in the area since its beginnings. Kamel was also responsible for giving me a unique experience: he conducted an interview with me for the Kuwaiti magazine *al-'Arabi* and, several months later, while back in Cairo, I was telephoned by my friend Mohamed Makhzangi, who works for the children's edition of the magazine, to say that he had a sum of money for me, my fee for the interview—the very first time I have been paid for giving an interview.

It is perhaps natural, having lived most of my life in Egypt, that I have given pride of place in my translating activities to Egyptian writers. The Arab world is made up of many countries, and it is difficult to keep up with what is being published in all of them. Where writers from Morocco, Algeria, and Tunisia are concerned there are many North Africans who are as familiar with French as they are with Arabic (some, like Taher Ben Jalloun, do their writing in French); it is therefore no surprise to find that many North African writers, hardly known in the rest of the Arab world, are available in French translation. When preparing my latest volume, I was happy to find an excellent story by a Tunisian writer named Brahim Dargouthi, whom I later discovered had been much translated into French, though this short story was his first appearance in English. From the works of Moroccan novelist and critic Mohamed

Barrada, who is a frequent visitor to Cairo, I translated his short story "Life by Installments," which appeared in an earlier volume of mine published by Quartet Books, where it drew the attention of several English critics. Another original North African writer worthy of mention is the Libyan Ibrahim al-Koni. I have made a point of including a story by him in the two volumes I have done since he came to my notice, and recently wrote to him—he lives in Switzerland—about translating his short novel *The Bleeding of the Stone*, only to find that someone was already working on it. Much of his work is in the process of being translated into German. It is surprising to me that in countries such as France and Germany more attention is given to translating modern Arabic fiction than in Britain and the United States. In Britain today, with Quartet Books having ceased to add new titles to their list, there is no single publisher available for such work, though Harvill Press has apparently opened its lists to fiction translated from the Arabic.

Among Egyptian writers I have translated is Mohamed El-Bisatie. Having long admired him as a writer of spare and telling short stories, it was natural that the first book I translated of his work was a representative volume of short stories. I was pleased to see, from a perceptive review by the Arabist Roger Allen, that his talents had not gone unnoticed. I followed this up with a short novel entitled *Houses behind the Trees*. El-Bisatie writes with great finesse and understanding of the narrow world in which he operates: village life around the area of Lake Manzala and the ordinary folk who make up its day-to-day life. No one, I feel, does this better than him. I was surprised to learn when I asked him whether he goes back to his village from time to time, that he has never been back since leaving it to come to university in Cairo. It is only recently that he has begun to widen his horizons and to write about Cairo, where he has made his home. For many years a friend—I enjoy his caustic remarks about situations and people—I have seen less of him for some time since retreating for the most part to my rambling house in a village outside Cairo. But we keep in touch by telephone and I am pleased that he seems to value my advice sufficiently to consult me about any new writing project he has in mind.

Another writer of whose stories I have published a representative volume is Said al-Kafrawi, under the title *The Hill of Gypsies*. He, too writes largely about peasant life, though so far he has restricted himself to the short story. He writes with a certain panache and attempts to endow the peasant with extra dimensions so that his stories are no longer mere depictions of a primitive way of life.

Mahmoud al-Wardani is a writer of talent on the Egyptian literary scene. I have translated several of his stories, and he came out to my village home in Fayoum to conduct a long interview with me for Cairo's literary review *Akhbar al-adab*. A short novel of his has now been chosen for translation and publication by the American University in Cairo Press. What, one asks, would modern Arabic literature in translation do without the efforts of the AUC Press, which has been responsible for thirty Mahfouz editions in English and more than fifty by other Arab writers?

Then there's my old friend Gamil Atia Ibrahim, who, in the early days, took himself off from Cairo to a teaching job in Asila, one of Morocco's unspoiled seaside resorts, about which he wrote a novel, simply entitled *Asila*, and then settled for life in Switzerland with his Swiss wife, working as a journalist and doing his creative writing in his spare time. I have translated stories of his that have appeared in anthologies, and one of his novels, *Down to the Sea*, was translated by Frances Liardet and published by Quartet Books.

Another writer whose stories I have translated and published is Yusuf Abu Rayya, whom I've known from the days of Yahya Taher Abdullah, when we were both friends of his. In December 2005 he was awarded the Naguib Mahfouz Medal for Literature for his novel *Wedding Night*, which has a deaf and dumb peasant as its central character. The novel is now being translated for publication by the AUC Press.

A writer of singular talent was Nabil Naoum Gorgy, who has now taken himself off to Paris and seems no longer to be writing, or at least publishing. Having spent time in New York, he has a knowledge of English and is well read in the less trodden byways of literature—the writings, for instance, of Jorge Luis Borges, Yasunari Kawabata, and the

Islamic Sufis. His somewhat offbeat stories with hints of the macabre have passed virtually unnoticed in Arabic, but I translated a volume of them that was published by Quartet Books under the title *The Slave's Dream* and received a laudatory notice in *The Observer*.

Gamal al-Ghitani, editor of *Akhbar al-adab*, is of course a major figure in the literary world and has had his novel *Zaini Barakat* translated into English by Farouk Abdel Wahab and published first by Penguin and more recently by the AUC Press. It has also been translated into several European languages. I included a short story by him in *Under the Naked Sky*.

Khairi Shalabi, also featured in *Under the Naked Sky*, has a vast output of writing. I was impressed by his *Wikalat 'Atiya*, a novel with the sort of 'local' background first presented by Naguib Mahfouz in such novels as *Midaq Alley* but with, to my mind, the advantage of having the dialog in the colloquial Arabic. It is a novel that deserves to be translated, and for a time I toyed with the idea of doing it myself, though I was daunted by its length. Now, though, having been awarded the Naguib Mahfouz Medal for Literature, it is being translated for publication by the AUC Press.

Mohamed Makhzangi has been a close friend ever since the day when he came and knocked on the door of my flat and introduced himself. Since then, he left Egypt to study medicine and alternative medicine in the Soviet Union and then to work on the magazine *al-'Arabi* in Kuwait. He is now back in Cairo and working on the children's edition of *al-'Arabi*. In the early days he was known for his extra short tales or sketches, often no more than a couple of hundred words, that encapsulated some pithy observation about a commonplace situation; of these I translated and published several. A powerful short story of normal length—a story ostensibly about a flight of ducks coming in to land on a lake, but with its own political message—is the first story in the volume *Under the Naked Sky*. He and I share an interest in animals.

Salwa Bakr is one of the growing number of women writers who today contribute to the literary scene in the Arab world. It is interesting to note that in my three volumes of stories from the Arab world, the first two, published in 1967 and 1983, each contained two women writers out of a total of twenty, while the latest volume, published in 2000, featured stories by eight women writers out of a total of thirty.

I remember first meeting Salwa many years back when she gave me a bundle of her stories in manuscript. We later met up at the Café Riche, a favorite haunt of Cairo's intellectuals, where I handed back her manuscripts and gave her what I thought might be helpful comments to some of the stories. However, I should have known that writers don't show their work other than for it to be praised—I myself am no different in this respect. What I also did not know at the time is that Salwa is renowned for being outspoken. "What are you?" she suddenly remarked, "a translator or a teacher of writing?" I got up and walked out of the café, convinced that this was the last I was to see of Salwa Bakr. She went off to Beirut and to Cyprus, and got in touch with me several years later on her return to Cairo, and it was then that I began putting together a collection of her stories in English translation. I recollect another encounter with her at a café, this time close to al-Azhar. We were sitting and discussing her stories and when we came to go she discovered that her coat, which she had taken off, had disappeared, stolen no doubt by the small boy who had come around offering combs for sale. I was struck, this time, by her remarkable sangfroid, accepting the loss with a mere shrug of the shoulders and the observation that the boy had been extremely adroit.

My volume of Salwa's stories was published by Quartet Books under the title *The Wiles of Men*. It did not do well (though it has now been taken up by the AUC Press), but I like to think that it opened the door for her to be published more extensively in translation, particularly in German.

Another woman writer whose work demanded to be translated was the Iraqi Buthayna al-Nasiri, who had made her home in Cairo. I produced a volume of her short stories, selected from the various volumes she had published in Arabic, with the AUC Press under the title *The Final Night*.

17

For some years now much of my time has been spent on writing children's books. My first interest in them came about when I was invited by a rich Syrian friend to spend a few days with him at his luxurious home in the south of Spain. One day we were sitting talking when his young son ran past. My friend called him over. He then inquired of the boy whether he knew about the Battle of Badr. The look on the boy's face told us the name rang no bell. One or two other questions showed that the boy knew next to nothing about his religion or its history. My friend explained to me that the boy was being educated at an English public school—Eton no less—but had no knowledge of Arabic or of Islam. As far as he knew there were no books in English about the Prophet's life that the boy could read. He asked me to write such a book, and mentioned a handsome fee that I would be paid.

I went away delighted with the commission that had fallen into my lap and immediately took myself off to the peace and quiet of my cottage in Kerry, bearing with me several Arabic books about the life of the Prophet and the early days of Islam. The project seemed to present no difficulty, but when I came to write it I had, perhaps for the first time in my life, what is known as 'writer's block,' and the more I sought to overcome it the more impossible the task appeared. Was it that I was being required to write a book for children, something I had never previously attempted? Perhaps my difficulty was compounded by the fact that my friend, being both generous and trusting, had been adamant about handing over to me then and there a check for the fee he had proposed, and I had banked the sum of money. I reached the stage when I felt there was nothing to do but sit down and write out my own check to my sponsor for the sum I had received. Eventually, though, I began to write various episodes of the book, and later strung them together into a life of the Prophet as seen through the main events of his life from birth to death.

On my return to London I handed the manuscript over to my sponsor and set about trying to find a suitable publisher for the book, and it was from this moment that my troubles started. Understandably, my sponsor wished to make sure that the book he had commissioned contained nothing that could be objected to, and he therefore had the book sent to an expert on the subject in Saudi Arabia. People who are asked to comment on a manuscript are only too happy when they find mistakes, while others, finding nothing to criticize, must of necessity come up with something to say against the book. In this case, the Saudi Arabian scholar instead of—for instance—objecting to the general tone of the book, pointed out several supposed glaring factual errors. My sponsor asked me to go and see him about the book and flung the report across the table at me. I was naturally taken aback, and being by nature diffident, I could only mumble that I was sure I hadn't made any such errors. Could it be that the many books I had read on the subject in English and Arabic had themselves contained factual errors? For my good fortune my friend Dr Ezzeddin Ibrahim, a scholar well versed in everything to do with Islam, and who had been professor of Arabic at Riyadh University and then the first vice- chancellor of the University of the United Arab Emirates, happened to be in London at the time. I took the report along to him. "The man's an ignoramus!" he told me, having read through the report, and he confirmed that in each and every instance it was I who was right and not the so-called expert. He also pointed out—something that in my state of confusion I had failed to notice—that the man's report contained no less than three grammatical errors! How, though, was I to persuade my sponsor that I, an Englishman, was right and his Saudi Arabian 'expert' wrong? In the end, I asked Ezzeddin whether he would very kindly come with me to see my sponsor. In this way, my sponsor was persuaded that the book I had written was free of error.

But my troubles with the book were not over. Having failed to find a British publisher for it, my sponsor gave it to Riad al-Rayyis, a Syrian friend of his who had a well-known bookshop in London and had also gone into publishing. I had already corrected the proofs of the book when Riad al-Rayyis decided to transfer to Beirut. Here the book was handed over to his local employees, who purported to correct mistakes I had made in English and reset it, making a real dog's dinner of it. My "Foreword," for example, was rendered "Forward," and on the map of Africa on the endpapers "Assyria" appeared instead of "Abyssinia." Thankfully, I don't believe the publisher ever made any attempt to sell the book; certainly I have never had any sales reports from him.

Bad as my experience was with my first book written for children, it perhaps paved the way for the time, several years later, when Neil Hewison at the AUC Press asked me whether I would be prepared to write two books for children with Egyptian backgrounds. He explained that he had a friend, Andy Smart, who was starting a publishing venture for children's books in English. When I went to see Andy, he told me that the British Council had promised to sponsor two titles if I were to write them. I was only too happy to agree, provided—I stipulated—that one of the books would be a collection of stories about the traditional wise-fool Goha, a character I have always enjoyed. In due course I wrote a book of Goha stories and another one of stories taken from traditional Egyptian folklore. It is interesting to note that the Arab world has never had any literature written specifically for children. Whereas in the west we think of *The Arabian Nights* as one of the great classics for children, it was by no means originally intended for children. When, for instance, I came to look up the stories for a book about Sindbad, I found much of the material quite unsuitable. In fact, *The Thousand and One Nights* (as it is more properly called), so lauded in the west, is not held in great regard by many Arabs.

And so began an association that produced no less than fourteen books, all of them illustrated by local Egyptian artists, and all renderings of stories from such works as *The Thousand and One Nights,* traditional Arab myths, and stories from Arab history, including books about the early days of Islam. I also wrote a second book of Goha stories. Andy ran the business—Hoopoe Books—with his Egyptian wife Nadia, and achieved good sales, several of the titles selling more than ten thousand copies. Even so, Hoopoe, particularly with the Egyptian pound steadily decreasing in value, could not provide him with the income he needed, with school fees for his two sons having to be paid in dollars, and he decided to return to Britain. Though Hoopoe Books puts out no new titles, the present ones continue to sell and to be reprinted.

In the meantime, wishing to go on writing children's books, I found in Dar el Shorouk, Egypt's leading publisher, a willingness to venture into publishing children's books in English, especially as Amira Abul-Magd, the wife of Shorouk's owner Ibrahim al-Muallim, who was in charge of the children's books side of the business, had lived for some of her life in the United States and was fluent in English.

To date, Shorouk has published some fifteen of my books, and prospects for sales seem to be improving. The books, as the earlier ones published by Hoopoe, are adaptations into English from Arab folklore—though there are two exceptions, both illustrated by an Italian artist. It happened that during one summer spent in Morocco, we escaped from the heat of Marrakesh to the seaside town of Essaouira, where I saw in one of the town's many art galleries some striking paintings of cats—animals that are close to my heart—done by Ruggero Giangiacomi. I met the artist and we agreed that if I wrote a children's book he would do the illustrations. Two days, later I came back with a short book called *The Cat and the Artist*, set among the fishing boats that lie in Essaouira's port. We then did a second book together called *The Acrobats of Marrakesh.*

When I first went to Essaouira I got to know a Dane called Frederic Damgaard, who had set up an excellent art gallery there. The gallery was devoted solely to a primitive art movement that he has been encouraging. The main figure in this movement was a certain Tabal, whom Damgaard actively promoted, and when it came to publishing a short booklet in English about the artist I was asked to do the translation. In my conversations with the gallery owner I had perforce to speak in French, a language full of grammatical traps for the foreigner. However it seemed that he felt I was up to the task and so I made my one and only translation from French—and was rewarded with a primitive picture by Tabal.

Some years back, Pat Gauch of Penguin/Putnam Books in New York was on holiday in Cairo visiting her daughter. She got in touch with me about a children's book that she wished to have translated from Arabic, and this led to her decision to do a book of Goha stories, with the novel idea of having the illustrations executed first of all in patchwork, an art that is practiced with skill in Cairo, and then photographed. The resultant book has now been published and has received encouraging notices.

In the meantime, friends of mine in Dubai, who had already set up there what must surely be the best bookshop in the Middle East, decided to venture into publishing, and we are now in course of sending to the printer the first four children's books with backgrounds of the Emirates and the Gulf.

18

My interest in animals stemmed from a childhood in which animals played perhaps a greater part than in the lives of most children. During my two years in Wadi Halfa in Sudan I was the proud owner of a donkey, and saw my parents riding about on horses and camels. I also recollect owning a rabbit and that we bred pigeons. Later, in Uganda, my father had a bulldog and my mother a parrot; we also had a monkey on a long chain, which had to be got rid of because of its inclination to bite anyone who attempted to pet it, and I myself had the first of many cats. My personal servant, Sherif, made me a series of catapults, which I employed against any birds that caught my attention. I later graduated to an airgun, and from there to a 2.2 rifle and a shotgun. Sherif also taught me how to snare birds, which I would incarcerate in home-made cages, where they fluttered about desperately until they gave up, clearly more interested in their freedom than all the food I tempted them with. At the school I went to in Kenya animals were also much in evidence—I remember the thrill of hearing a lion roar down on the playing fields and being told that one of the masters had set off to shoot it. When playing in the wild bush that surrounded the school, we would often put up a deer. Butterfly collecting was a favorite hobby of the boys, and this extended to various sorts of insects, as well as the large, evil-looking trapdoor spiders whose homes littered the playing-fields: they were easily tickled out of their homes with a length of grass and then quickly wrapped in a handkerchief and tipped into a killing bottle. A memory from those days still haunts me as, one evening, some of us boys were gathered around a collection of various insects that had been pinned out on a board. Suddenly, to my horror, I saw a large trapdoor spider, having spent insufficient time in the killing bottle, heave itself up from the board and walk across the desk, its body still pierced through by a large, brightly-topped pin. The wretched creature was soon swept up in a handkerchief and given a second period in the killing bottle. I have always been frightened of spiders, more so than by snakes, and this particular scene has remained vividly with me; this and the memory of all the birds that I killed for the sheer excitement of it.

I don't read French with ease but something prompted me some years ago to read a short piece by a French Orientalist, pointing out that of all the revealed religions Islam showed the greatest concern for animals; it ended by noting that no one had as yet made a proper study of the subject. I therefore sought out those passages of the Qur'an (no less than five of whose chapters are named after animals) that had anything to say about animals. From there I went to the Hadith, and was rewarded to find that this literature contained a large number of stories commending kindness to a variety of animals. I then found that the great al-Jahiz had written a book called quite simply *Kitab al-hayawan* ('The Book of Animals') and that al-Damiri had also written a comprehensive book on the subject. I was of course already aware of the entertaining stories contained in *Kalila wa Dimna*, a book of animal fables, which had been translated from Persian into Arabic and added to, becoming a classic of Arabic literature. And subsequently I came across a work entitled *The Case of the Animals against Man*, written by the Brethren of Purity in Baghdad in the tenth century.

The random slaughter of birds that I was responsible for as a boy brings to mind the Hadith of the Prophet that states, "He who kills a sparrow uselessly, it cries out to God on the Day of Resurrection and says:

'O Lord, Your servant killed me uselessly and not for any benefit.'" I have thus acquired a certain sense of guilt toward animals, a guilt that perhaps can be partly assuaged by attempting to do something in the cause of animals as and when I can. I thus made an adaptation into English of *The Case of Animals against Man,* under the title *The Island of Animals*. It was published, together with an introduction I wrote about Islam's teachings regarding man's responsibilities toward animals, by Quartet Books. It was excellently printed and was beautifully illustrated by the Tunisian artist Sabiha Khemir. But it was received by general critical silence, except for an appreciative review by Tom Porteous, an Arabist whom I was known to, and one other review by someone who, having praised my work in other fields, questioned why I should waste my time on such a subject! It did, however, get taken up in the United States, where a paperback edition was published by the University of Texas Press.

Later, when I began publishing children's books with Hoopoe Books in Cairo, I produced a children's book entitled *Animal Tales from the Arab World*, which included stories from *The Arabian Nights* and *Kalila wa Dimna*, as well as from a small collection of stories with the delightful title *The Superiority of Dogs over Many of Those Who Wear Clothes*.

19

I continually promise myself, with each book translated, that it will be the last, and yet, like the nicotine addict, I find myself returning to the habit. Having made the major decision to leave Cairo and go to live in Morocco, I sat down and added up the number of books I had translated from modern Arabic literature: it came to twenty-eight. I was able to persuade myself that I should round it up to thirty, especially when a friend got in touch in Cairo and brought me a large anthology devoted to the Moroccan short story. I have therefore started collecting material for a volume of Moroccan short stories and am trying to interest a publisher in the project before starting work. Also, as I mentioned earlier, I feel it is high time someone produced a volume of stories from the Emirates in translation—and the publishing house that has recently been established in Dubai by friends of mine, the Abulhoul family, has agreed to produce such a volume. (Abdullah Abulhoul was chief of police in Dubai; he is now retired but is as active as ever with a variety of interests, including a date plantation outside Dubai from which, with every visit there, we leave with large quantities of the best local dates, known as Barhi. His English wife, Isobel, and their son Mansour are active with the bookshops and the publishing venture.) With volumes like these, one of the difficulties is reading the work of the writers and then making a choice. My task in this respect on the Emirates volume is being considerably lightened by my Egyptian friend Kamel Yusuf Hussein, a distinguished journalist and translator from Dubai, who has agreed to supply me with the necessary volumes and to help me in my selection.

Also on my plate is the book of selections from the Holy Qur'an, arranged under subject matter, that my friend Ezzeddin Ibrahim and I have been engaged on these last few years. Perhaps, too, we may well venture on a fourth volume of Hadith literature. At the same time I hope to produce the occasional children's book.

The possibility that I might one day give time to being a translator was clearly with me from fairly early days. Idly looking through some old papers recently, I came across an article on "Translation and Translators" I had published in the London-based magazine *al-Adab wa'l-fann* in 1946, that is, before I myself had had any translations published. Re-reading the article, I find that it expresses the very same thoughts that I still have on the subject, some sixty years later. Where would the cultural world be without its translators? How is it that we have all had access to Homer and the writings of the ancient Greeks, to books such as *The Epic of Gilgamesh*, to the Russians, Cervantes, Proust, Pessoa, and so on. Who, I ask in my article, having read the works of writers such as Dostoyevsky, remembers the name of Constance Garnett, the woman who was responsible for translating so much of early Russian literature? I point out that translation is an art that requires considerably more than simply having a knowledge of two different languages. I also mention that some of the world's great literary figures have not found it beneath them to turn their hands to translation. Among such writers are Baudelaire, who translated some of the work of Edgar Alan Poe into French—in fact, so little success did he have as a poet during his lifetime that he would often proudly describe himself as "the translator of Poe." Even the great Proust began his literary career by translating some of the writings of Ruskin. Then there is D.H. Lawrence, who translated Giovanni Verga's novel *Mastro Don Gesualdo* from the Italian, and so on. The early Arabs, it seems, showed greater appreciation for their translators; it is recorded that in early Abbasid times the famous Honein ibn Ishaq was paid a handsome monthly salary and that the caliph Ma'mun rewarded him with the weight in gold of the books he had translated. I find myself stressing in that 1946 article, as I do today, that translation is not simply a matter of putting one word in place of another. It is an art, and, as someone once said: "Nothing moves without translation."

Index